Hans Kelsen Memorial Lectures
on International Peace and Security Law

edited by

Prof. Dr. Dr. h.c. Dr. h.c. Claus Kreß LL.M. (Cambridge),
University of Cologne

Volume 3

David Kretzmer

The Law and Politics of Belligerent Occupation

The Case of the West Bank

Nomos

C.H.BECK

INSTITUTE FOR INTERNATIONAL PEACE AND SECURITY LAW

The Deutsche Nationalbibliothek lists this publication in the Deutsche Nationalbibliografie; detailed bibliographic data are available on the Internet at http://dnb.d-nb.de

ISBN 978-3-7560-3302-7 (Print)
978-3-7489-6077-5 (ePDF)

Online Version
Nomos eLibrary

1st Edition 2025

Preface

This study is based on the Eighth Hans Kelsen Memorial Lecture on International Peace and Security that I was honoured to deliver at Cologne University on 3 July 2024. I wish to thank my friend and colleague, Professor Claus Kreß, for inviting me to deliver the lecture, and for his understanding regarding the need for changes in the time of the lecture after war broke out in my part of the world. Professor Kreß' work on the use of force and the law of armed conflict has made a major contribution to our understanding of these important issues. I have benefited greatly from our frequent exchange of views on these issues, especially in times of crisis when one needs to discuss the issues with a person of impeccable academic integrity and expertise.

The work of Hans Kelsen played an important part in my legal education. My professor of constitutional law, Professor Hans Klinghoffer, wrote his doctorate under the guidance of Professor Kelsen, before Kelsen moved from Vienna to Cologne. In our lectures on jurisprudence Kelsen's pure theory of law was part of the legal thought of our professors, almost all of whom had received their legal education in Europe before WWII. Kelsen's contribution to international law and his views on peace and security are well-known. While during his life time many scholars were sceptical about his vision of a greater place for judicial action as a means of enforcing international law, with the recent rate of activity of the ICJ and the ICC, we are seeing part of Kelsen's vision in action.

The longstanding conflict between Israel and the Palestinians is a burning issue in international peace and security that has concerned the international community for many decades. Public attention at the time of the lecture was concentrated on the October 7 Hamas attack on Israel and the subsequent war in Gaza. At the time of writing the war continues after the collapse of a temporary cease-fire that led to return of some Israeli hostages being held in Gaza in exchange for release of Palestinian prisoners in Israel. The loss of life, destruction and human suffering that have been caused in this armed conflict are immense. One hopes that the cease-fire will be renewed and that it will lead to an end to the conflict and to opening a new chapter in the relations between Israel and the Palestinians.

Sadly the war between Israel and the Hamas was one more round in a never-ending series of violent confrontations between Israel and the

Palestinians. Despite the urgency of the situation I did not address this issue in my lecture and shall not be addressing it in this study. Rather I concentrate on an issue that is not unconnected and remains a central issue in the Israel-Palestinian conflict - the continued occupation of the West Bank by Israel. The international community has expressed its deep concern over this issue on innumerable occasions. As was made clear in the Advisory Opinion of the International Court of Justice that was published shortly after I delivered the lecture, the international community regards continuation of the occupation as violation of the prohibition on acquiring territory through use of force, frustration of the right to self-determination of the Palestinian people, and a major obstacle to peace in the Middle East.

In this study I do not dwell on the views of the international community; rather I discuss the way the Israeli authorities have related to the occupation, and more specifically to the interplay between law and politics. I show how lawyers changed or circumvented the law in order to cater to political interests and how judges adopted tactics to avoid having to decide on the legality of government policies and practices. This leads me to some searching questions about the law of belligerent occupation in the modern world.

Sources

The judgments of the Supreme Court that are cited in this study are all available online in the Nevo database. Other than the few instances in which I have referred to the official report of the case, I have provided only the case number, names of the main parties and the date of the judgment. The judgments of the Court are in Hebrew: English translations of some of the cases are available on the site of the Israel Supreme Court (at https://supreme.court.gov.il/sites/en/Pages/home.aspx) and the site of the Israeli Supreme Court Project of Cardozo Law School (at https://versa.cardozo.yu.edu/).

Acknowledgments

I wish to thank Professor Kreß and his wonderful team for hosting me and my partner when we were in Cologne for the lecture. I found the meeting with the team in the seminar Professor Kreß arranged after my lecture to be highly stimulating. The comments and questions of the participants gave me much room for thought.

Thanks also to my research assistant, Avishag Bartuv, who provided comments on the draft of this study, and worked tirelessly on checking the sources and the footnotes.

Jerusalem, April 2025

Table of Contents

Introduction

In the last fifteen years there has been a growing literature on the law of belligerent occupation. In the English language at least five books have been written on the general subject, alongside dozens of articles discussing various aspects of this branch of law.[1] This academic interest in the law of occupation might appear somewhat baffling, since most commentators accept that while there have been quite a number of cases of belligerent occupation since WWII, there are very few, if any cases, in which the occupying power has conceded that it is indeed bound by this body of law.[2]

In many cases the occupying power simply denies that the territory seized by use of force is occupied territory, claims that the territory is its own, or annexes the territory under its domestic law.[3] In other cases the occupying power argues that the law of occupation that forbids the occupying power from changing the legal and political regime in the territory is inappropriate, since it is imperative to impose a regime change in the occupied country.[4] In yet other cases the occupying power claims that it used force in order to protect the population in the occupied territory from

---

1 Yoram Dinstein, *The International Law of Belligerent Occupation* (2nd edn, CUP 2019); Eyal Benvenisti, *The International Law of Occupation* (2nd edn, OUP 2012); Aeyal Gross, *The Writing on the Wall: Rethinking the International Law of Occupation* (CUP 2017); Yutaka Arai-Takahashi, *The Law of Occupation: Continuity and Change of International Humanitarian Law, and Its Interaction with International Human Rights Law* (Martinus Nijhoff 2009); Eliav Lieblich and Eyal Benvenisti, *Occupation in International Law* (OUP 2022). This list does not include books written specifically about the territories occupied by Israel. See, eg, Orna Ben-Naftali, Michael Sfard and Hedi Viterbo (eds), *The ABC of the OPT: A Legal Lexicon of the Israeli Control over the Occupied Palestinian Territory* (CUP 2018).

2 Benvenisti (n 1) ch 7; Peter MR Stirk, *The Politics of Military Occupation* (Edinburgh University Press 2009) ch 1. For a useful site analysing the international status of occupied territories see the Rule of Law in Armed Conflicts of the Geneva Academy:<https://www.rulac.org/> accessed 22 January 2025 (hereinafter Rulac).

3 eg Moroccan attitude to West Sahara: Sven Simon, 'Western Sahara' in Christian Walter and others (eds), *Self-Determination and Secession in International Law* (OUP 2014) 255; Russian attitude to Crimea and to Donbass region of Eastern Ukraine: Rulac, (n 2) <https://www.rulac.org/browse/conflicts/military-occupation-of-ukraine#collapse2accord> accessed 8 January 2025; Iraqi occupation of Kuwait: Benvenisti (n 1) 170.

4 eg US occupation of Iraq: ibid 249 – 275.

an oppressive regime[5] or that it used force to gain control over the occupied territory at the invitation of the legitimate government of that territory.[6] In other cases the occupying power claims that there is an independent state in the occupied territory.[7]

There is one apparent, though, highly ambiguous exception to the above scheme of things: the occupation by Israel of the territories it occupied in the 1967 Six Day War. It is this occupation that is the focus of this study.

The UN Security Council has held on numerous occasions that Israel's policies in the occupied territories are an obstacle to a political solution to the Israel-Palestine conflict, thus threatening peace and security in the Middle East.[8] Soon after I delivered the Hans Kelsen Memorial Lecture on which this study is based, the International Court of Justice (ICJ) delivered its Advisory Opinion on *The Legal Consequences Arising from the Policies and Practices of Israel in the Occupied Palestinian Territory*.[9] In its Advisory Opinion the ICJ expressed the long-held view of the international community that Israel's prolonged occupation of the West Bank involves violation of the prohibition on acquiring territory through use of force and of the right to self-determination of the Palestinian people.

In this study I shall not be discussing the latest ICJ Advisory Opinion, nor the legality of Israel's policies and practices under international law that

5 eg Vietnamese occupation of Cambodia: ibid 185; Turkey occupation of Northern Cyprus: Iocovos Kareklas, 'International Law on the Turkish Military Intervention: The Argument from the Treaty of Guarantee' *University of Oxford, Strategy, Statecraft, Technology: Changing Character of War* (14 July 2022) <https://static1.squarespace.com/static/55faab67e4b0914105347194/t/62d01ffa55951d03df9a7ed4/1657806843466/Iacovos+Kareklas+-+International+Law+on+the+Turkish+Military+Intervention+of+Cyprus.pdf> accessed 2 January 2025.

6 eg Russian occupation of Afghanistan: Benvenisti (n 1) 177.

7 eg Turkish recognition of Turkish Republic of Northern Cyprus (TRNC): Rulac (n 2) <https://www.rulac.org/browse/conflicts/military-occupation-of-cyprus-by-turkey#collapse2accord> accessed 8 January 2025. While Turkey justified its 1974 invasion and occupation of northern Cyprus on the need to protect the Turkish minority on the island (Kareklas (n 5)) in 1983 it recognized the self- proclaimed TRNC; Russian occupation of Abkhazia and South Ossetia: Rulac (n 2) <https://www.rulac.org/browse/conflicts/military-occupation-of-georgia-by-russia#collapse2accord> accessed 8 January 2025.

8 See, eg, UNSC Res 446 (22 March 1979) UN Doc S/RES/446(1979); UNSC Res 465 (1 March 1980) UN Doc S/RES/465(1980); UNSC Res 2334 (23 December 2016) UN Doc S/RES/2334(2016).

9 *Legal Consequences Arising from the Policies and Practices of Israel in the Occupied Palestinian Territory, Including East Jerusalem* (Advisory Opinion) [2024] ICJ Rep 186 (hereinafter: Advisory Opinion, *Occupied Palestinian Territory*).

are addressed in the Opinion.[10] Rather I shall dwell on the way the Israeli authorities have related to the occupation, and more specifically on the interplay between law and politics in their relation to the occupation. I shall show how lawyers changed or circumvented the law in order to cater to political interests and how judges adopted tactics to avoid having to decide on the legality of government policies and practices. We will see that in the end politics gained the upper hand over law. This will lead me to some searching questions about the role of lawyers in the public service and the law of belligerent occupation in the modern world.

10 For some initial reactions to the Advisory Opinion see <https://verfassungsblog.de/category/debates/the-icj-advisory-opinion-on-the-occupied-palestinian-territory-debates/> accessed 8 January 2025.

Chapter 1: Historical Background

1.1 Beginnings of Political Zionism

The conflict between Israel and the Palestinians did not begin with the occupation in 1967 of territories held by the surrounding Arab states. It can be traced back to the end of the 19th Century when Jews began to arrive in Palestine, not as immigrants, but as settlers determined to find a national solution to what was known as the "Jewish question". The rise of political Zionism, and the creation of the Zionist movement by the Austro-Hungarian visionary, Theodor Herzl, inevitably led to a clash with the local majority Arab population in Palestine who saw themselves threatened by the Zionist project.[11] Faced with a worsening situation of pogroms and endemic discrimination in Europe, Zionist settlers were concerned with finding a solution to their own plight, and not with the implications for the local Arab population of their programme of establishing a state for the Jews in a land that they regarded as their ancestral homeland. In the colonial era at the fin de siècle, in which the self-determination of peoples had not yet become recognized as a guiding political, let alone legal, principle, the Zionists placed their hopes in support of the colonial powers of the day.

For various political reasons that will not be discussed here, the Zionist demands met with support from Great Britain, one of the two leading colonial powers of the era (the other being France).[12] The Balfour Declaration of November 1917, the creation of the Mandate system, and the subsequent decision of the victorious Principal Allied Powers to grant the Mandate over Palestine to Britain and to incorporate the Balfour Declaration in it, were major milestones both in the Israel-Palestine conflict and in the involvement of the international community in that evolving conflict.[13]

---

11 For a study of the early years of Zionism see Neville J Mandel, *The Arabs and Zionism Before World War I* (University of California Press 1976).

12 For a discussion on the events that led to British support for the Zionist project see Jonathan Schneer, *The Balfour Declaration: The Origins of the Arab-Israeli Conflict* (Random House 2010); David Cronin, *Balfour's Shadow: A Century of British Support for Zionism and Israel* (Pluto Press 2017) 4-14.

13 For a detailed description of events leading to establishment of the State of Israel see Alan Dowty, *Israel/Palestine* (4th edn, Polity Press 2017); Benny Morris, *Righteous Victims: A History of the Zionist-Arab Conflict, 1881-2001* (Vintage Books 2001); Ian

1.2 British Mandate over Palestine

Britain occupied Palestine in December 1917 and ruled Palestine from 1923 under a League of Nations Mandate. The legal aspects of the Mandate will be discussed below. For the moment we note that under the Mandate, Britain undertook to put into effect the commitment in the Balfour Declaration for "establishment in Palestine of a national home for the Jewish people", while at the same time doing "nothing ... which might prejudice the civil and religious rights of existing non-Jewish communities in Palestine, or the rights and political status enjoyed by Jews in any other country".[14] As the Arab inhabitants of the land had not been asked for their opinion on the Mandate, and the British were fully aware that had they been asked they would have totally rejected the idea,[15] from the start the British placed themselves in a situation of conflicting and irreconcilable demands of the two main communities in Palestine. Throughout the whole period of the Mandate (1923-1948) the Zionists demanded allowing free immigration of Jews and the right to purchase land for their settlement, while the Arabs strongly opposed both demands.[16]

With the rise of Nazism in Germany, Jews were desperate to escape Europe. The doors of the U.S. and Canada were closed to them and many found their home in Mandatory Palestine.[17] Thus, while according to a census

---

Black, *Enemies and Neighbours: Arabs and Jews in Palestine and Israel, 1917-2017* (Atlantic Monthly Press 2017). For the Palestinian view of these events see Edward Said, *The Question of Palestine* (Vintage Books 1992); Rashid Khalidi, *The Hundred Years' War on Palestine* (Metropolitan Books 2020).

14 British Mandate Over Palestine (1922) <https://www.jewishvirtuallibrary.org/text-of-the-british-mandate-for-palestine> accessed 8 January 2025.

15 See Victor Kattan, *From Coexistence to Conquest: International Law and the Origins of the Arab-Israeli Conflict 1891-1949* (Pluto Press 2009) 121.

16 For further discussion of the Mandate years and the conflicting demands on the British see Christopher Sykes, *Crossroads to Israel* (Indiana University Press 1973); Naomi Shepherd, *Ploughing Sand: British Rule in Palestine 1917-1948* (Rutgers University Press 2000); Tom Segev, *One Palestine, Complete: Jews and Arabs under the British Mandate* (Picador 2000).

17 On the restrictive immigration policy of the U.S., beginning in the 1920's and continuing during the 1930's and WWII, see the site of the United States Holocaust Memorial Museum <https://encyclopedia.ushmm.org/content/en/article/immigration-to-the-united-states-1933-41> accessed 8 January 2025; Bat-Ami Zucker, 'American Refugee Policies in the 1930s' in Frank Caestecker and Bob Moore (eds), *Refugees from Germany and the Liberal European States* (Berghahn Books 2010) 151. On the Canadian policy see Irving Abella and Harold Troper, *None Is Too Many: Canada and the Jews of Europe 1933-1945* (University of Toronto Press 2012).

carried out by the British, in 1931 there were 174,606 Jews in Palestine, who comprised about 16.9% of the total population, by 1941 their number had grown to 474,202, who now comprised 30% of the total population.[18] The large influx of Jewish immigrants and purchasing of land for Jewish settlement led to the Arab revolt against the British Mandate authorities (1936-1939).[19]

Faced with the deteriorating situation in Palestine and conflicting demands of the Zionist leadership and the local Palestinian Arabs, in 1937 the British government established a Royal Commission to look into the position and suggest a solution. After intensive hearings in Palestine, the Commission, headed by Lord Peel, reached the conclusion that the Mandate was not workable, and that the two communities – Jews and Arabs - could not live together in one state. The Commission therefore recommended partition of the country: a Jewish state would be established in a small part of the country and the Arabs in the other part would be joined with what was then Transjordan. There would be a transfer of populations, involving a small number of Jews who lived outside the area to be allocated to the Jewish state, and a large number of Arabs who lived in that area.[20]

The Peel Commission plan was totally rejected by the Palestinian Arabs. They saw it as a violation of their right to their country and a breach of the British commitment when it received the Mandate from the League of Nations that there would not be a Jewish state in Palestine, there would be no land expropriation and no expulsions of population.[21] The Zionist

18 See "Population of Palestine by Religions" in A Survey of Palestine, Prepared in December 1945 and January 1946 for the information of the Anglo American Commission of Inquiry, Vol. 1, 141 <https://www.bjpa.org/content/upload/bjpa/a_su/A%20SURVEY%20OF%20PALESTINE%20DEC%201945-JAN%201946%20VOL%20I.pdf> accessed 8 January 2025.

19 On the Arab revolt see Oren Kessler, *Palestine 1936: The Great Revolt and the Roots of the Middle East Conflict* (Rowman and Littlefield 2023); Segev (n 16) Part II; Morris (n 13) 128-160.

20 The full report of the Peel Commission is available at <https://ecf.org.il/media_items/290> accessed 8 January 2025.

21 Due to the apprehension of the Arab inhabitants, a short time before the Mandate over Palestine was approved by the League of Nations Council, the British Colonial Secretary, Winston Churchill, issued a White Paper in which he attempted to allay Arab concerns without backing down from the commitment in the Balfour Declaration. Churchill made it clear that there was no intention to make the whole of Palestine Jewish, but only to found a Jewish home in Palestine. The existing Jewish community would be extended so that "it may become a centre in which the Jewish people as a whole may take, on grounds of religion and race, an interest and a pride."

leadership was split over the very idea of partition. Nevertheless, while all rejected the concrete proposals of the Peel Commission, the Zionist Congress took a pragmatic approach and authorised the Zionist Organisation Executive to enter into negotiations "with a view to ascertaining the precise terms of HM Government for the proposed establishment of a Jewish State."[22]

The British government initially expressed support for the Peel Commission's proposals, but it soon reversed course and established the Woodhead Commission. The Commission was encouraged to bury the partition proposal, and it proceeded to do so.[23] Nevertheless, while rejected at the time, the Peel Commission's partition proposal set the tone for the political "solution" to the conflict between Jews and Arabs in Palestine that was to be adopted after WWII and is to this day the favoured solution of the international community.

After WWII, when the horrors of the Holocaust were revealed, British Foreign Secretary Ernest Bevin announced creation of the Anglo-American Commission of Inquiry.[24] The Committee's task was to examine the situation of Jewish refugees in Europe and to consult with Arabs and Jews in Palestine on the conditions there, and the possibility of allowing large-scale Jewish immigration, as well as to make recommendations to the British government on both an interim arrangement and a political settlement in Palestine. Members of the Commission visited displaced persons' camps in Europe and the Commission held hearings in Washington, Palestine and Cairo in which both Arab and Zionist representatives presented their case. In its report of April 1946 the Commission recommended that the British

---

British White Paper of June 1922 <https://avalon.law.yale.edu/20th_century/brwh1922.asp> accessed 8 January 2025.

22 On the Peel Commission's recommendation of partition, and the developments following publication of its report, see TG Fraser 'A Crisis of Leadership: Weizmann and the Zionist Reactions to the Peel Commission's Proposals, 1937-8' (1988) 23 *Journal of Contemporary History* 357.

23 ibid. The Palestine Partition (Woodhead) Commission Report (1938) is available at <https://archive.org/details/WoodheadCommission/page/n5/mode/2up> accessed 8 January.

24 The background and mandate of the Commission are described in the Commission's Report at <https://avalon.law.yale.edu/subject_menus/angtoc.asp> accessed 8 January 2025. Also see statement of President Truman on establishment of the Commission: 'Statement by the President Concerning the Anglo-American Committee of Inquiry (Palestine Commission)' (10 December 1945) <https://www.trumanlibrary.gov/library/public-papers/210/statement-president-concerning-anglo-american-committee-inquiry-palestine> accessed 8 January 2025.

grant certificates for entry of 100,000 Jewish refugees into Palestine. While it refrained from making specific recommendations on the future government of the country, the Commission categorically rejected the notion of partition into two states. It opined that any future arrangement for rule of the country should be based on three principles:

> "I. That Jew shall not dominate Arab and Arab shall not dominate Jew in Palestine. II. That Palestine shall be neither a Jewish state nor an Arab state. III. That the form of government ultimately to be established, shall, under international guarantees, fully protect and preserve the interests in the Holy Land of Christendom and of the Moslem and Jewish faiths."

The Commission's recommendation on immigration faced strong opposition of the British government. However, US President Harry Truman supported the recommendation,[25] and appointed a Cabinet Committee to assist him in considering the Commission's proposals.[26] This led to appointment of the joint British-US Morrison-Grady Committee. This Committee rejected many of the Peel Commission's recommendations and accepted a British plan for dividing the country into provinces that would remain under British trusteeship.[27] President Truman initially backed this plan, but later tended to support partition of the country.

After WWII ended the Zionist underground movements began a campaign of armed resistance to further British control over Palestine. The resistance intensified after Foreign Secretary Bevin refused to implement the Anglo-American Commission recommendation to allow 100,000 Jewish refugees to enter the country. The Jewish underground movements were also involved in bringing Jewish refugees from Europe to Palestine despite the British ban on immigration.[28]

---

25 'Statement of the President on Receiving the Report of the Anglo-American Commission of Inquiry' (30 April 1946): <https://www.trumanlibrary.gov/library/public-papers/92/statement-president-receiving-report-anglo-american-committee-inquiry> accessed 8 January 2025.

26 Statement by President Truman: 'Immigration into Palestine' (4 October 1946) <https://avalon.law.yale.edu/20th_century/decad163.asp> accessed 8 January 2025.

27 See Memorandum of Ambassador Grady (24 July 1946): <https://ecf.org.il/media_items/1019> accessed 8 January 2025.

28 For a succinct description of this "illegal immigration", known as "Aliyah Bet," see United States Holocaust Memorial Museum, 'Aliyah Bet' (USHMM Encyclopedia, 7 April 2021) <https://encyclopedia.ushmm.org/content/en/article/aliyah-bet accessed 8 January> 2025.

1.3 United Nations Partition Resolution

As conditions in Palestine deteriorated and violence increased, Britain announced that it was relinquishing the Mandate and handing the matter to the United Nations. In May 1947 the UN General Assembly appointed the United Nations Special Committee on Palestine (UNSCOP), to examine the causes of the conflict in Palestine, and if possible, to recommend a solution.[29] UNSCOP, made up of the representatives of 11 states, spent 5 weeks hearing testimony in Palestine. The Zionists flooded the Committee with testimony, while the Palestinian Arab leadership boycotted the Committee. When they visited Palestine, Committee members witnessed the refusal of the British to allow entrance into Palestine of 4500 Jewish Holocaust survivors who had set sail to Palestine aboard the refugee ship named *Exodus*. The forced return of the ship to Europe and the subsequent detention of the refugees in a camp in Germany had a huge impact on public opinion and, it would seem, on some members of the Committee too.[30]

In the report that it submitted at the end of August 1947 UNSCOP recommended unanimously that the British Mandate should end, and that Palestine should become independent.[31] However, on the future government of Palestine the Committee was split. Eight of the eleven members recommended partition of Palestine into two independent states, a Jewish state and an Arab state, that would be joined in an economic union. Jerusalem and its environs would not be part of either state, but a *corpus separatum*, under international control.[32] The Committee attached a map of Palestine with the recommended borders of the two states and of the corpus separatum.[33] While the recommendation was for a Jewish state, in the territory that was to be allotted to that state the Jews would be a bare majority (600,000 Jews and 475,000 Arabs).

The three minority members (from India, Persia and Yugoslavia) rejected the idea of partition. They recommended an independent federal state that

---

29 UNGA Res 106 (15 May 1947).

30 David Horowitz, *State in the Making* (Knopf 1953) 178-179.

31 UNGA 'Report of the United Nations Special Committee on Palestine' UNGAOR 2nd Session Supp No 11 UN Doc A/364 (3 September 1947) ch V, Section A. Available at: <https://www.jewishvirtuallibrary.org/united-nations-special-committee-on-palestine-unscop> accessed 22 January 2025 (hereinafter: UNSCOP Report).

32 ibid ch V, Section B.

33 The map is available at <https://www.un.org/unispal/document/auto-insert-208958/> accessed 8 January 2025.

would be established after a preparatory period under an authority decided upon by the General Assembly. The minority members were convinced that partition could not create two viable states, that the federal solution would force co-operation between Jews and Arabs, and that it was "the only practical and workable approach."[34]

The UN General Assembly set up an ad hoc Committee on Palestine to hear the views of Palestinian Arabs and Zionists on the UNSCOP recommendations.[35] The Palestinian Arabs expressed total opposition to partition, which they saw as a violation of their right, as the majority in Palestine, to establishment of an independent state that would respect the rights of all minorities. The Zionists, on the other hand, while dissatisfied with the boundaries of their proposed state and the fact that Jerusalem would not be part of it, accepted partition, which they saw as fulfilment of their aspiration for an independent Jewish state. Britain refused to express its views on the future government of Palestine and announced that it would be leaving Palestine by mid-August 1948 (later changed to mid-May of the same year).

On 29 November 1947, in GA Res 181, the General Assembly decided by a two-thirds majority, both to approve the Britain's decision to end the Mandate and to adopt the partition proposal of the UNSCOP majority.[36] The Zionists were jubilant that there would now be a Jewish state that would enjoy international legitimacy; the Arabs rejected the GA resolution and decided to use violence in order to prevent partition.[37]

1.4 1947/8 War and Establishment of the State of Israel

Immediately following adoption of GA Res 181 war broke out in Palestine between Arabs and Jews. At first the Arabs went on the offensive and the Zionist organizations, especially its main armed force, the Hagana, were mainly on the defensive, but due to better organisation by April 1948 the Hagana went on the offensive.

---

34 UNSCOP Report (n 31) ch VII.

35 The records of the Ad Hoc Committee may be found at <https://www.un.org/unispal/document-source/general-assembly-ad-hoc-committee-on-the-palestinian-question/page/2/> accessed 8 January 2025.

36 UNGA Res 181(ii) (29 November 1947) UN Doc A/RES/181(II).

37 Avi Shlaim, *War and Peace in the Middle East, A Concise History* (Penguin Books 1994) 22.

It was during this period that large numbers of Palestinians left their homes.[38] Many were forced to leave by the Hagana and other Zionist militias; others fled the dangers of war, hoping to return to their homes when the fighting stopped.[39] By the time the British left Palestine on 15 May 1948, the Hagana had gained control over most of the areas allotted to the Jewish state in the Partition Resolution, and had even expanded its control over Jaffa, the main Arab town in Palestine.

In the afternoon of Friday, 14 May 1948, the leaders of the Jewish community in Palestine declared the establishment of a Jewish state, to be called the State of Israel, that would come into existence on the termination of the Mandate at midnight. The Declaration on the Establishment of the State of Israel, signed by the 37 members of the Provisional State Council of the Jewish community, stated that the state was established "by virtue of our natural and historic right and on the strength of the resolution of the United Nations General Assembly..."[40] Following the terms of GA Res 181, the Declaration promised that the new state would foster development of the country for the benefit of all its inhabitants and would ensure "complete equality of social and political rights to all inhabitants [of the state] irrespective of religion, race or sex; guaranteed "freedom of religion, conscience, language, education and culture"; and affirmed that the State would safeguard the Holy Places of all religions and would be faithful to the principles of the Charter of the United Nations. It also appealed to the Arab inhabitants of the State "to preserve the peace and participate in the upbuilding of the State on the basis of full, and equal citizenship and due representation in all its provisional and permanent institutions."

On 15 May 1948, the day that the Mandate ended and Israel was established, the armies of five surrounding Arab states invaded the territory of Mandatory Palestine and full-scale war broke out with the newly formed Israel Defence Forces (IDF). During the course of the War the IDF expanded the territory allotted to the Jewish state under the GA Partition Plan.

---

38 Rashid Khalidi, 'The Palestinians and 1948: The Underlying Causes of the Failure' in Eugene L Rogan and Avi Shlaim (eds), *The War for Palestine: Rewriting the History of 1948* (CUP 2001) 12–13.

39 For the most comprehensive discussion of the reasons the Arabs left or were expelled from their homes see Benny Morris, *The Birth of the Palestinian Refugee Problem Revisited* (2nd edn, CUP 2004).

40 State of Israel, *The Declaration of the Establishment of the State of Israel* (14 May 1948) <https://www.gov.il/en/pages/declaration-of-establishment-state-of-israel> accessed 8 January 2025.

Following a series of UN Security Council resolutions ordering a truce and negotiations between the parties,[41] the war ended in 1949 with the signing of armistice agreements between Israel and four of the Arab states that had invaded Palestine: Egypt, Jordan, Syria and Lebanon.[42]

Under the armistice agreements the territory of the Palestine Mandate was divided into three parts. Israel had control over more territory than the territory allotted to the Jewish state under the UN Partition Plan; Jordan controlled what became known as the West Bank, and Egypt had control of the Gaza Strip. Jerusalem, which was supposed to be a corpus separatum, was a divided city. Jordan had control over the eastern part, including the Old City and the holy places, while Israel had control over western Jerusalem. Approximately 700,000 Palestinian Arabs who had lived in areas that were now in control of the IDF had fled or been expelled from those areas. An early decision of the Provisional Government of Israel was that Arabs who were no longer in the territory controlled by the IDF would not be allowed to return to their homes. The defeat and displacement of the Arabs who had lived in the territory that was now part of Israel are known to Palestinians as the *Naqba* (the catastrophe).

1.5 Armistice Agreements

The armistice agreement between Israel and Egypt states that the Demarcation Line established between the parties "is not to be construed in any sense as a political or territorial boundary, and is delineated without prejudice to the rights, claims and positions of either Party to the Armistice as regards ultimate settlement of the Palestine question."[43]

The Armistice with Jordan does not contain a similar clause. It does, however, state that:

1. The principle that no military or political advantage should be gained under the truce ordered by the Security Council is recognized;

---

41 UNSC Res 54 (15 July 1948) UN Doc S/RES/54(1948); UNSC Res 60 (29 October 1948) UN Doc S/RES/60(1948); UNSC Res 61 (4 November 1948) UN Doc S/RES/61(1948); UNSC Res 62 (16 November 1948) UN Doc S/RES/62(1948); UNSC Res 66 (29 December 1948) UN Doc S/RES/66(1948).

42 No armistice or other agreement has ever been signed between Israel and Iraq, the fifth Arab state involved in the 1948 war.

43 *Israel-Egypt Armistice Agreement 1949* (signed 24 February 1949, Jewish Virtual Library) art V.2 <https://www.jewishvirtuallibrary.org/israel-egypt-armistice-agreement-1949> accessed 8 January 2025.

2. It is also recognized that no provision of this Agreement shall in any way prejudice the rights, claims and positions of either Party hereto in the ultimate peaceful settlement of the Palestine question, the provisions of this Agreement being dictated exclusively by military considerations.[44]

Following the signing of the Armistice Agreement with Jordan there was uncertainty about the legal status of the Armistice lines between Israel and Jordan. On the one hand, the Agreement states that its provisions are "dictated exclusively by military considerations", thereby seemingly implying that those lines are only the dividing lines between two armies, and not lines defining the political borders of the State of Israel. On the other hand, both sides to the Agreement committed themselves to refrain from use of force against the other. They recognized the right of each party to its security and to be free from attack by the other party and declared that "establishment of an armistice between the armed forces of the two Parties is accepted as an indispensable step toward the liquidation of armed conflict and the restoration of peace in Palestine."[45]

The Armistice lines reflected the situation on the ground when the cease-fire demanded by the UN Security Council came into effect. Under these lines Israel had more territory than the territory allotted to the Jewish state under the UNSCOP Partition Plan that was adopted in UNGA Res. 181(II). Since it feared that there may be pressure to force it to withdraw to the Partition Plan lines, Israel had a political interest in promoting recognition of the Armistice lines as its political border.[46] Pursuing this interest, quite

44 *Israel-Jordan Armistice Agreement* (signed 3 April 1949, Jewish Virtual Library) art II <https://www.jewishvirtuallibrary.org/israel-jordan-armistice-agreement-1949> accessed 8 January 2025.

45 ibid art I.

46 Israel's fears of pressure to withdraw to the Partition Resolution lines were not unfounded. At one stage in late 1948 President Truman was of the opinion that if Israel refused to relinquish control over the Negev that had been allocated to the Arab state, in exchange for recognition of its control over the Galilee that was allocated to the Arab state, he would demand full implementation of the Partition Plan. See Michael J Cohen, *Truman and Israe*l (University of California Press 1990) 260. Also see Hagai Eshed, '10 Years of Israel's Foreign Policy: "Continuing the War of Independence by Other Means"' *Davar* (13 April 1958) 14. The fear that there would be pressure to return to the Partition lines, or at least to relinquish control over some of the territory not included in the Jewish state under the Partition Resolution, was a constant concern of Israeli decision makers. See, eg, the briefing of Minister of Foreign Affairs, Moshe Sharett, to the Israeli delegation to the 1949 Lausanne Conference convened by the UN Conciliation Commission for Palestine (UNCCP). Sharett explained that the Armistice Lines serve as a barrier against attempts to

soon after the end of the War in 1949, senior officials presented arguments that the Armistice lines were the recognized borders of the Jewish state. A main example is a letter dated 23 October 1949 from Shabtai Rosenne, legal adviser of the Israel Ministry for Foreign Affairs, to Abba Eban, head of Israel's delegation to the UN, in which Rosenne argued that Israel has sovereignty over all the territory that is under its control. According to Rosenne, this sovereign territory includes West Jerusalem, which, under Resolution 181, was supposed to be part of the corpus separatum that would not belong to either of the two states that would come into being in Palestine after the Mandate ended.[47] Rosenne subsequently published an article in which he argued that the Armistice Lines were Israel's political borders.[48] As legal adviser to the Israel Ministry of Foreign Affairs, it is inconceivable that Rosenne would have publicly presented a view on the State's borders that was incompatible with the view of his government.

There is also some academic support for the view that the Armistice Lines are the political borders of the State of Israel. In his book on the Creation of States in International Law James Crawford argued that Israel was "effectively and lawfully created as a State by secession from Palestine in the period 1948 to 1949. Its original territory was the armistice territory, not the partition territory".[49] Yoram Dinstein reached a similar conclusion based on his reading of the Armistice Agreements as treaties that recognized the borders of Israel.[50] In its Advisory Opinion in the *Wall* case, the ICJ also

---

reduce the territory of the state or in some other way to change the borders of the state without its consent. *Foreign Ministry documents*, Book 4, Item 146, 307-308. Also see the cable of a Foreign Ministry official to the Ministry Director General in which he reports on a meeting with a senior USA official who said that Israel would have to relinquish control over some of the territory that was not allocated to her under UNGA Res 181, ibid Item 149, 316-317. The Foreign Ministry documents are available at <https://search.archives.gov.il/search/0b0717068893ebe1> [in Hebrew] accessed at 8 January 2025.

47 Foreign Office document FO/I/31452(19).

48 Shabtai Rosenne, *Israel's Armistice Agreements with the Arab States: A Juridical Interpretation* (Tel Aviv 1951). Referring to the Armistice Lines with Jordan, Rosenne wrote: "It is possible, however, that the juridical function of these lines is far greater, and that they are indistinguishable from international frontiers proper." (ibid 47).

49 James Crawford, *The Creation of States in International Law* (2nd edn, OUP 2006) 434.

50 Yoram Dinstein, 'The Arab-Israeli Conflict from the Perspective of International Law' (1994) 43 *University of New Brunswick Law Journal* 301.

implicitly recognized the Armistice Lines as the political borders of the sovereign State of Israel.[51]

1.6 The Uneasy Peace

From 1949 until 1967 an uneasy peace existed between Israel and the surrounding states, broken in 1956 by the Sinai campaign in which, under a secret agreement between Israel, France and Great Britain, Israel gained control over the Sinai Peninsula and Gaza.[52] Under pressure from the U.S. and USSR Israel was forced to withdraw from all the territory it had taken. Given the veto power of France and Great Britain the UN Security Council was unable to act and the matter passed to the UN General Assembly. Under a series of resolutions, the General Assembly established the UN Emergency Force (UNEF) to secure and supervise the cessation of hostilities.[53] As this was not a peace-enforcement force created by the UN Security Council under Chapter VII of the UN Charter, it could only operate with the consent of the states concerned. After the withdrawal of the IDF from Sinai in March 1957, UNEF remained in Sinai with the consent of the Egyptian government and patrolled the border between Israel and Egypt.[54]

On the initiation of the Arab League, in 1964 Palestinian exiles created the Palestinian Liberation Organization (PLO). Its Charter, named the

51 Eyal Benvenisti, 'In Hague the Green Line was established: The UN Court for the first time recognized the right of Israel to exist in the 1948 borders' *Ha'aretz* (12 July 2004). This recognition of the Armistice Line as Israel's border is also implicit in the Advisory Opinion of July 2024 (n 9) in which the ICJ made a clear distinction between the status of the territory east of that Line as occupied territory, and the territory of Israel west of the Line. This recognition of the Armistice Line as Israel's border is also implicit in the various UN resolutions relating to recognition of the State of Palestine in the territory occupied by Israel in 1967. See, eg, UNGA Res 58/292 (5 May 2004) UN Doc A/RES/58/292; UNGA Res 66/225 (22 December 2011) UN Doc A/RES/66/225.

52 On this campaign see Motti Golani, *Israel in Search of War: The Sinai Campaign 1955-1956* (Liverpool University Press 2013).

53 UNGA Res 997 (2 November 1956) UN Doc A/RES/997(ES-I); UNGA Res 998 (4 November 1956) UN Doc A/RES/998(ES-I); UNGA Res 999 (4 November 1956) UN Doc A/RES/999(ES-I); UNGA Res 1000 (5 November 1956) UN Doc A/RES/1000(ES-I); UNGA Res 1001 (7 November 1956) UN Doc A/RES/1001(ES-I); UNGA Res 1002 (7 November 1956) UN Doc A/RES/1002(ES-I); UNGA Res 1003 (10 November 1956) UN Doc A/RES/1003(ES-I).

54 United Nations, *UNEF I Background* (UN Peacekeeping 2011) <https://peacekeeping.un.org/en/mission/past/unef1backgr1.html> accessed 8 January 2025.

Palestinian National Charter, declared that Palestine under the borders of the British Mandate is one indivisible unit, that only the Jews who had normally lived in Palestine before the "Zionist invasion" would be allowed to remain there, that armed struggle is the only way to liberate Palestine, and that "commando action constitutes the nucleus of the Palestinian popular liberation war."[55]

None of the Arab states recognized Israel and the relations between Israel and the surrounding Arab states, Egypt, Jordan, Syria and Lebanon were based on the Armistice Agreements that were monitored by Mixed Armistice Commissions under the auspices of the UN Troup Supervision Organization. The Commissions considered complaints of the parties on violations of the Armistice Agreements and reported to the UN Security Council. As there was a dispute between Israel and Syria over the competence of the Commission to consider complaints relating to demilitarized zones that had been part of Palestine but were under Syrian control, Israel refused to attend meetings of the Israel-Syria Commission.

1.6 June 1967 "Six Day War"

The events that led to the June 1967 War have been dealt with at length in the literature.[56] The following description, taken from previous work of the present writer,[57] is based on the Israeli perception of these events.[58] This perception is important since it provides part of the explanation of Israel's policies in the West Bank after the end of that war.

On 15 May 1967 Egypt reinforced its infantry and armed forces in Sinai on Israel's southern border. The following day, Egyptian President Jamal Abd Al-Nasser demanded of United Nations Secretary-General, U Tant, that the United Nations (UN) withdraw its Emergency Force, placed on the Israel-Egypt border in the wake of Israel's 1957 withdrawal from Sinai. On the same day two Egyptian armoured divisions were sent into Sinai

---

55 The English translation of the Charter may be found at the Avalon Project: <https://avalon.law.yale.edu/20th_century/plocov.asp> accessed 8 January 2025.

56 Michael Oren, *Six Days of War: June 1967 and the Making of the Modern Middle East* (OUP 2002); Guy Laron, *The Six Day War: The Breaking of the Middle East* (Yale University Press 2017).

57 David Kretzmer and Yaël Ronen, *The Occupation of Justice: The Supreme Court of Israel and the Occupied Territories* (2nd edn, OUP 2021) ch 1.

58 For a different perception see John Quigley, *The Six Day War and Israeli Self-Defense: Questioning the Legal Basis for Preventive War* (CUP 2013).

as reinforcement for the 70,000 Egyptian soldiers and members of the Palestinian Liberation Army already there. A few days later Egypt imposed a blockade on the passage of Israeli ships through the Straits of Tiran, and on 30 May it signed a defence pact with Jordan. All these steps were accompanied by constant declarations by Nasser and the Arab press about impending war that would lead to Israel's destruction.

The Egyptian moves took Israel's political leaders by surprise. The general consensus among Israel's political leadership was that diplomatic steps should be taken to find a political solution to the crisis. However, as the crisis deepened, especially after the blockade of the Straits of Tiran, fear grew among almost all of the political parties represented in the *Knesset* and the general public that Israel's very existence was threatened, and that if a political solution were not found, military force would have to be used to meet the threat.

During the period between 15 May and the outbreak of war on 5 June (known in Israel as the "waiting period"), the government reinforced the armed forces by calling up the reserves. At the same time it sought a political solution to the crisis, first and foremost by international action to lift the blockade on Israeli navigation. Under public pressure the government was broadened to include members of the main opposition bloc, *Gahal*, and General Moshe Dayan was appointed minister of defence, a position held until then by Prime Minister Levi Eshkol.[59]

The diplomatic talks bore little fruit. Despite international resolutions in favour of free navigation and a specific guarantee given by the United States to Israel regarding freedom of shipping in the Straits of Tiran and the Suez Canal, the United States, Britain, and France were not prepared to take effective measures to lift the blockade or to reduce the threat to Israel. The USSR was openly hostile to Israel and supportive of the Arab countries. On 4 June 1967 the government decided to take military action to meet the threat on the Egyptian border. This decision enjoyed wide public and political support. In the *Knesset* debate that took place on the day that the War started, all parties supported the government's policy, with the sole exception of the pro-Moscow New Communist List (*Rakakh*).

---

59 Dayan was IDF chief-of-staff at the time of the 1956 Sinai Campaign and had later served as minister of agriculture. In 1967 he was a member of *Knesset* on behalf of the opposition *Rafi* Party.

With the benefit of hindsight, it is possible to identify wider historical factors that led to the 1967 crisis.[60] It may be questioned whether President Nasser really intended going to war. Yet there is little doubt that at the time, the military leadership, the main political parties, and virtually the entire Jewish public in Israel perceived the situation as one that imposed a serious threat to the State of Israel. Israel's borders, set by 1949 Armistice Agreements with the surrounding states, had left the country vulnerable to attack. Israel is minute in size (at some points the distance between the Armistice Line with Jordan and the Mediterranean Sea is less than ten kilometres), and there was genuine fear that if it did not act, it would be attacked simultaneously on a number of fronts, and that this could lead to a catastrophe.[61]

The initial aim of military action in 1967 was the removal of the threat that had been posed by Egypt's massing of forces in Sinai, removal of the UN Emergency Force, and blockade on Israeli shipping in the Straits of Tiran. Once the War began, further aims developed that had been neither part of the original plan of action nor defined in advance by the Cabinet. In the days preceding the War, a message was sent to King Hussein of Jordan, promising that if Jordan refrained from military action against Israel in the event of hostilities between Israel and Egypt, Israel would not attack Jordan. Nevertheless, after hostilities began between Israel and Egypt, Jordanian artillery started firing on West Jerusalem. Another urgent message was sent to King Hussein urging him to cease fire, but the artillery fire continued. After Jordanian forces occupied the UN Truce Supervision Organisation (UNTSO) headquarters located on a hill in the southern part of Jerusalem, the order was given to mount a counterattack, and full-scale war ensued on the eastern front. Although there had been no initial plan to conquer the whole of Jerusalem and the West Bank, the War had a dynamic of its own. Within two days, Israeli forces had taken the Old City of Jerusalem and gained control over the whole of the West Bank. At the same time, Israeli forces in the south took the Gaza Strip and the

60 For a retrospective analysis of the events that led to the War see Richard B Parker (ed), *The Six-Day War: A Retrospective* (University Press of Florida 1996); Laron (n 56).

61 The clearest manifestations of the anxiety, shared by the political leadership and the public, were the preparations made during the waiting period to cope with expected casualties. Fourteen thousand hospital beds and thousands of coffins were prepared and municipal parks were turned into potential burial grounds: see Yossi Goldstein, *Eshkol—Biography* (Keter Publishing 2003) 565 [in Hebrew].

Sinai Peninsula. They later conquered the Golan Heights. Thus began the occupation.

Chapter 2: Managing the occupation

2.1 Initial Political Decisions

The tension and fear that the Israeli public had suffered in the "waiting period" had an enormous influence over the public and political attitudes to Israel's control over the territories it had occupied in the war. Most Jewish citizens were convinced that Israel should not be prepared to relinquish control over these territories unless peace agreements were reached that would eliminate, or at least diminish, the vulnerability of Israel to future attacks. This was reflected in the political discussions that commenced a short time after the war ended. In these discussions there was consensus that all territories taken should be retained until peace agreements with the neighbouring states were concluded. However, divergent views within the Cabinet emerged regarding the future status of the West Bank and Gaza. While occupying the West Bank had not been an initial war aim, there had always been both political and military circles that believed that Israel, the Jewish state, should have control over the whole of the historical Land of Israel.[62] They now regarded what had happened as an historic opportunity to realise this vision. Within a short time, claims were made that the territories taken in the war had not been occupied, but were parts of the homeland, liberated from foreign occupation.

Numerous discussions on Israel's policy towards the newly occupied territories were conducted in the Cabinet Committee on Security and subsequently in the full Cabinet. These discussions culminated in a formal resolution on those matters on which it was possible to reach consensus in

62 The Zionist Revisionist movement had always claimed the right of the Jewish people to sovereignty over the whole of the historic land of Israel. This view was represented in the Knesset by the Herut Party, which was the main party in the opposition"Gahal" bloc at the time of the 1967 war. It's leader, Menachem Begin, became a member of the National Unity Government that was formed a few days before the war. The programme of Gahal, published before the Knesset elections in 1965 stated: "The Herut movement will continue to present the view among the nation of the whole of the homeland, namely the right of the Jewish people over the Land of Israel, in its historic entirety, an eternal right that is beyond challenge." The programme is available at <https://www.idi.org.il/media/6443/%D7%92%D7%97%D7%9C-1965.pdf> accessed 8 January 2025.

the National Unity Government. According to this resolution, which initially remained secret, Israel would be prepared to offer peace treaties to Egypt and Syria based on the international border that existed between those states and Mandatory Palestine.[63] This meant that Gaza, which had been under Egyptian military rule since 1948, would remain in Israeli hands. No mention was made of the future of the West Bank. From records recently released it appears that there was wide consensus amongst members of the Cabinet that Israel should retain some form of permanent control over the West Bank and Gaza.[64]

On one question there was wide political agreement: the future of Jerusalem. Soon after the battle subsided, the Cabinet decided on immediate application of Israeli law and administration in the eastern part of the city, including the Old City, which had been conquered in the War.[65] At the government's initiative the *Knesset* (Israel's parliament) amended the Law and Government Ordinance. This amendment stated that the law, jurisdiction, and administration of the state would apply to any part of the Land of Israel designated by the government.[66] The government subsequently published a decree in the Official Gazette applying the state's law, jurisdiction, and administration in East Jerusalem. In 1980 the Knesset passed the Basic Law: Jerusalem the Capital of Israel. Section 1 of this Basic Law declares that the "complete and united Jerusalem is the capital of Israel."[67]

---

63 Avi Raz, *The Bride and the Dowry, Israel, Jordan and the Palestinians in the Aftermath of the June 1967 War* (Yale University Press 2012) 43-47. For the Cabinet discussions that culminated in this resolution see *Minutes of the 18-19 June 1967 Cabinet meetings* (Israel State Archives) <https://catalog.archives.gov.il/chapter/protocols-18-19-june-1967/> [in Hebrew] accessed 8 January 2025.

64 Omri Shefer Raviv, *The Creation of Israeli Control over the Palestinian Population in the West Bank and Gaza Strip, 1967-1969* (DPhil thesis, Hebrew University of Jerusalem, September 2019).

65 From 1948–1967 Jerusalem was a divided city: the western part was controlled by Israel and the eastern part, including the Old City, by Jordan. On the decisions relating to Jerusalem after the 1967 War see Meron Benvenisti, *Jerusalem, The Torn City* (University of Minnesota Press 1977); Amnon Ramon with the Participation of Yaël Ronen, *Residents, Not Citizens: Israeli Policy towards the Arabs in East Jerusalem, 1967–2017* (Jerusalem Institute for Policy Research 2017) 15–67.

66 *Law and Government Ordinance, 1948 (Amendment No 10)*, 1967, which added Article 11B.

67 *Basic Law: Jerusalem, Capital of Israel* (1980) <https://m.knesset.gov.il/EN/activity/documents/BasicLawsPDF/BasicLawJerusalem.pdf> accessed 8 January 2025.

2.2 Milestones in the Occupation

In the years that have passed since it began in June 1967 there have been a number of milestones in the occupation.[68] During the initial period, Israel allowed the Palestinians to manage their own affairs while clamping down and using repressive measures against Palestinians who resisted the occupation, even when the means of resistance were non-violent (such as commercial strikes). There was some armed resistance in the West Bank and Gaza and this met with a forceful reaction. Measures against Palestinian leaders who encouraged non-cooperation with the military authorities included deportations to Jordan and later to Lebanon.[69]

A special section is devoted below to the settlement policy, that began shortly after the war ended in June 1967. On the basis of a government decision, the military commander used his power under international law to seize property for military needs in order to gain control over land that was then used for Israeli settlements. In the first decade of the occupation, during which the Labour Party was in power, the settlements were established in the Jordan valley and in locations close to the Green Line, especially in the Jerusalem area.[70] A new era in the settlement policy began after the Likud Party won the elections in 1977 and a new government headed by Menachem Begin was formed.

During the years significant changes were introduced by military orders into the local law, some in order to meet local needs, others to promote Israeli interests.[71] There was freedom of movement between the West Bank, Gaza and Israel and many Palestinians from the occupied territories worked in Israel.

Under the Peace Agreement between Israel and Egypt (1979) Israel dismantled the settlements that it had established in the Sinai Peninsula after 1967 and withdrew its forces to the international border between Egypt

---

68 For detailed discussion of the history of the occupation see Ahron Bregman, *Cursed Victory: Israel and the Occupied Territories: A History* (Penguin Books 2015); Neve Gordon, *Israel's Occupation* (University of California Press 2008).

69 For the measures taken against Palestinian leaders who were not prepared to co-operate with the military authorities see Shefer Raviv (n 64).

70 For the settlement policy during the first decade of the occupation see Gershom Gorenberg, *The Accidental Empire: Israel and the Birth of the Settlements, 1967-1977* (Times Books 2006).

71 On the major changes in the local law in the first twenty years of the occupation see Raja Shehadeh, *Occupier's Law: Israel and the West Bank* (rev edn, Institute for Palestine Studies 1988).

and Palestine. It retained control over the West Bank and Gaza and those parts of the Golan Heights that had remained in its hands after an interim agreement reached with Syria after the 1973 Yom Kippur War. Under the Peace Agreement with Egypt, Israel agreed to hold talks over granting autonomy to the Palestinians in the West Bank and Gaza. These talks broke down after Israel invaded Lebanon in 1982.

In 1987 the first *intifada* (uprising) broke out in the West Bank and Gaza. The military authorities reacted with numerous harsh measures, including curfews and other restrictions on freedom of movement, wide-scale administrative detentions, punitive house demolitions and use of force in dispersing demonstrations.[72] In response to the continuing violence and following the 1991 Gulf War, the U.S. and USSR sponsored the Madrid Conference for Peace in the Middle East.[73] At Israel's insistence the Palestinians could not participate in this conference as a separate delegation, but a delegation of Palestinians from the West Bank and Gaza were part of the joint Jordanian-Palestinian delegation.[74]

The Madrid conference did not lead to any agreements. However, in 1992 elections brought the Labour Party to power, and a new government headed by the Party's leader Yitzchak Rabin was formed. This government decided to negotiate with the PLO, recognized internationally as the legitimate representative of the Palestinian people. These negotiations led to the Oslo Accords and subsequent agreements between Israel and the Palestinians.[75]

Under the Oslo agreements the West Bank was divided into three areas, labelled A, B and C. The Palestinian Authority, established under the agreements, was given control over Area A, which includes the West Bank Palestinian cities. In Area B Israel retained security control, while the Palestinian Authority was responsible for services to the Palestinian inhabitants. Israel retained control over Area C, in which all the Israeli settlements were located and which constitutes 60% of the territory of the West Bank. Israel also retained security control over all Israelis in the West Bank, including

72 See Zeev Schiff and Ehud Ya'ari, *Intifada: The Palestine Uprising – Israel's Third Front* (Ina Friedman ed, Simon and Schuster 1990); Aryeh Shalev, *The Intifada: Causes and Effects* (Westview Press 1991); Edgar O'Ballance, *The Palestine Intifada* (Macmillan 1996); Bregman (n 68) 145-156.

73 ibid 167; Dowty (n 13) 143-145.

74 ibid.

75 On the Oslo Accords see Geoffrey R Watson, *The Oslo Accords: International Law and the Israeli-Palestinian Peace Agreements* (OUP 2000).

those who entered Area A. The Palestinians had control over most of Gaza, not including the areas in which Israeli settlements had been established.

Under the Oslo Accords final status talks on the future of the West Bank and Gaza were supposed to be concluded within five years. The agreements stated that in the interim period neither side would do anything to change the status of the territories. At the same time, under the agreements the issue of Israeli settlements was supposed to be dealt with in the final status negotiations.

For a number of reasons, the Oslo Accords did not operate as planned.[76] The final status negotiations did not take place, but in July 2000 the Israeli prime minister, Ehud Barak, and the PLO chairman, Yasser Arafat, met at Camp David in a summit under the auspices of US President Bill Clinton.[77] After these talks broke down, violence broke out in the occupied territories, in what became known as the second *intifada*.[78] The level of violence and counter-violence in this *intifada* destroyed the faith of many Israelis and Palestinians in a peaceful resolution to the conflict between the two peoples.[79]

---

76 For differing analyses of why the Oslo Accords did not lead to peace see Aharon David Miller, 'Why the Oslo Peace Process Failed' *Foreign Policy* (13 September 2023) <https://foreignpolicy.com/2023/09/13/oslo-accords-1993-anniversary-israel-palestine-peace-process-lessons/> accessed 8 January 2025; *Explainer: The Oslo Accords* (Institute for Middle East Understanding) <https://imeu.org/article/explainer-the-oslo-accords> accessed 8 January 2025; Avi Shlaim, 'The Rise and Fall of the Oslo Peace Process' in Louise Fawcett (ed), *International Relations of the Middle East* (OUP 2005) ch 11; Shlomo Ben Ami, 'The slow, tragic death of the Oslo Accords' *The Strategist* (28 September 2023) <https://www.aspistrategist.org.au/the-slow-tragic-death-of-the-oslo-accords/> accessed 8 January 2025.

77 There is a large literature on the Camp David talks between Israeli Prime Minister Ehud Barak and PLO Chairperson Yasser Arafat, and some controversy over what actually happened there and why the talks broke down. See, eg, Ian S Lustick, 'Camp David II: The Best Failure and its Lessons' (2001) 16 *Israel Studies Bulletin* 1; Clayton E Swisher, *The Truth about Camp David: The Untold Story of the Collapse of the Middle East Peace Process* (Nation Books 2004); Raymond G Helmick, *Negotiating outside the law: Why Camp David failed* (Pluto Press 2004); Shlomo Ben Ami, *Prophets without Honor: The 2000 Camp David summit and the end of the two-state solution* (OUP 2022); Aharon David Miller, 'Lost in the Woods: A Camp David Retrospective' *Carnegie Endowment for International Peace and Security* (13 July 2020) <https://carnegieendowment.org/posts/2020/07/lost-in-the-woods-a-camp-david-retrospective?lang=en> accessed 8 January 2025.

78 See Bregman (n 68) 247-267.

79 Zohar Palti, 'The Implications of the Second Intifada on Israeli views of the Oslo Process' *FIKRA Forum* (8 September 2023) <https://www.washingtoninstitute.org/

Suicide bombings and other terrorist attacks in Israel led the government to decide on construction of a separation barrier in the West Bank. While the formal and initial reasons for this decision were security considerations, namely making it more difficult for potential terrorists from the West Bank to enter Israel, there is little doubt that some of the persons involved in planning and supporting construction of the barrier had political motives too.[80] Some considered that building the barrier would be the first step in separating Israelis and Palestinians into two states; others thought that the barrier could include territories in the West Bank on the Israeli side of the barrier, thereby creating facts that would influence future negotiations on a two-state solution. Construction of the barrier and creation of a special regime in the area surrounding it caused massive harm to many Palestinians communities.[81] The consequences of constructing the barrier were the subject of an Advisory Opinion of the International Court of Justice[82] and of over a hundred petitions to the Israel Supreme Court.[83]

Israelis had settled in the Gaza Strip since the late nineteen seventies. As the number of attacks against settlers and IDF soldiers grew, Ariel Sharon, who was elected prime minister in 2001, decided in 2004 on the "Disengagement Plan" under which the 7000 settlers would be removed from the Gaza Strip and the IDF would withdraw its forces from the area.[84] After approval by the government and the Knesset this plan was implemented in 2005 and the IDF proclaimed that it was no longer responsible for affairs in Gaza.[85] The "Disengagement Plan" also included withdrawal of settlements in a small section in the northern part of the West Bank.

In 2006 elections were held by the Palestinian Authority and the Hamas movement gained a majority of votes. In 2007 violence broke out between the Hamas and Fatah forces in Gaza. The Hamas managed to defeat the Fatah and took control over the whole of Gaza.[86]

---

policy-analysis/implications-second-intifada-israeli-views-oslo> accessed 8 January 2025.

80 Kretzmer and Ronen (n 57) 237-239.

81 ibid 235-237.

82 *The Legal Consequences of the Construction of a Wall in the Occupied Palestinian Territory (*Advisory Opinion) [2004] ICJ Rep 131 (hereinafter: *Wall* Advisory Opinion).

83 Kretzmer and Ronen (n 57) 240-272.

84 ibid 163-165.

85 IDF, Proclamation on end of military government (12 September 2005).

86 On Hamas' path to power in Gaza see Björn Brenner, *Gaza Under Hamas: From Islamic Democracy to Islamic Governance* (I.B. Tauris 2016) ch.2.

Following the withdrawal of settlers and IDF personnel from Gaza, there was uncertainty as to the status of the area.[87] Although there was no longer Israeli military presence in the area, Israel maintained strict control over its border with the area, over the airspace and access to and from the sea. After the Hamas took control over the area and fired rockets into Israel, the Israeli authorities placed severe restrictions on movement of people and goods to and from Gaza. Until the Hamas attack of 7 October 2023 and the subsequent war in Gaza there was a huge debate about the status of Gaza as occupied territory.[88]

87 The different views on this question are presented by Michal Luft, 'Living in a Legal Vacuum: The Case of Israel's Legal Position and Policy towards Gaza Residents' (2018) 51 *Israel Law Review* 193 and Aeyal Gross (n 1) 204.

88 Those who argued that Gaza remained occupied territory include Yoram Dinstein (n 1) 296-303; Shane Darcy and John Reynolds, 'An Enduring Occupation: The Status of the Gaza Strip from the Perspective of International Humanitarian Law' (2010) 15(2) *Journal of Conflict & Security Law* 211; Sari Bashi and Kenneth Mann, 'Control and Responsibility: The Legal Status of the Gaza Strip after the "Disengagement"' (2011) 14 *Hamishpat* 35 [in Hebrew]; Nicholas Stephanopoulos, 'Israel's Legal Obligations to Gaza After the Pullout' (2006) 31 *Yale Journal of International Law* 524; Mustafa Mari, 'The Israeli Disengagement from the Gaza Strip: an End of the Occupation?' (2005) 8 *Yearbook of International Humanitarian Law* 356; Iain Scobbie, 'Gaza', in Elizabeth Wilmshurst (ed), *International Law and the Classification of Conflicts* (OUP 2012) 280. Those who held otherwise include Yuval Shany, 'Faraway, So Close: The Legal Status of Gaza after Israel's Disengagement' (2005) 8 *Yearbook of International Humanitarian Law* 369; Elizabeth Samson, *Is Gaza Occupied? Redefining the Legal Status of Gaza* (Begin-Sadat Center for Strategic Studies 2009) <https://besacenter.org/mideast-security-and-policy-studies/is-gaza-occupied-redefining-the-legal-status-of-gaza-3-2/> accessed 8 January 2025; Benvenisti (n 1) 211-212. And see Aeyal Gross (n 1) who argues against a binary approach and advanced the notion of "functional occupation."

Chapter 3. Legal Approach to the Occupation

3.1 International Law of Belligerent Occupation

The international law of belligerent occupation, as set out in the Hague Regulations attached to the Convention (IV) Respecting the Laws and Customs of War on Land, 1907 (Hague Regulations) and Geneva Convention IV Relative to the Protection of Civilian Persons in Time of War, 1949 (GCIV), rests on a number of principles. In the first place, since the occupying power has attained effective control over the area, it cannot leave a governmental vacuum. It therefore has the obligation to fulfill the most fundamental obligation of any government: ensuring public order and civil life. The occupying power may protect its military interests in the occupied territory, but it must find a balance between those needs and the interests of the local population. Occupation is a temporary regime, dictated by the fortunes of war, and the occupying power does not gain sovereignty over the occupied territory. Hence it may not change the law in the territory unless it is absolutely necessary to do so in order to protect its military needs or to promote the benefit of the local population.[89]

Both the Hague Regulations and GCIV place significant restrictions on the authority of the occupying power in occupied territory. Private property must be respected and the occupying power must act as a trustee of public property: it may enjoy the fruits of such property but it may not appropriate the property itself. The power of the occupying power to take security measures against local inhabitants, defined under GCIV as "protected persons",[90] is restricted. It may not deport them or forcibly transfer them in the occupied territory itself,[91] unless their temporary evacuation is required for their own security or for imperative military reasons.[92] If the occupying power considers it necessary for imperative reasons of security, it may, at the most, subject protected persons to assigned residence or

89 Hague Regulations (1907) art 43; Benvenisti (n 1) 91-94; Yoram Dinstein, 'Legislative Power in Occupied Territories' (1973) 2 *Iyunei Mishpat* 505 [in Hebrew].

90 Geneva Convention IV, art 4.

91 ibid art 49.

92 ibid art 49, para 2.

internment.[93] Under Art 49(6) of GCIV it is forbidden for the occupying power to transfer part of its own civilian population into the occupied territory.

3.2 Initial Approach of Israeli Military Lawyers

On the day the Israel Defence Forces (IDF) gained control over the West Bank in June 1967, the IDF military commander issued two proclamations and one military order. The proclamations stated that the IDF had taken control over the area, that all governmental power in the area was concentrated in the military commander's hands, and that the prevailing law in the area would remain in force, subject to any changes introduced by military orders.[94] The military order defined security offences and established military courts to try persons charged with committing such offences. The order included a provision stipulating that the military courts must comply with the provisions of the Fourth Geneva Convention (GCIV), and that in case of a clash between that Convention and military orders the Convention would prevail.[95]

The military proclamations and order had been prepared during the nineteen-sixties by the IDF MAG's office in contingency files prepared for any future war that might take place between Israel and the surrounding Arab states.[96] The MAG at the time was Lt Colonel Meir Shamgar, who was later to become Attorney General of Israel, a justice of the Supreme Court, and president of that Court. The assumption in preparing these proclamations and orders was that any territory outside Israel's existing borders that would be taken by the IDF in the case of a war with the neighbouring states would be occupied territory in which the IDF would be bound by the international law of belligerent occupation.

That this was indeed the MAG's assumption was confirmed one month after the June 1967 War ended when Mr Shamgar appeared before a Knes-

---

93 ibid art 78.

94 Proclamation No. 2 On Law and Administration (7 June 1967) (English translation available in Shamgar (n 96) 450).

95 *Security Provisions Order (West Bank(1967*, art 35. Similar orders were promulgated relating to the other territories taken in the war.

96 Meir Shamgar, 'Legal Concepts and Problems of the Israeli Military Government - The Initial Stage' in Meir Shamgar (ed), *Military Government in the Territories Administered by Israel 1967-1980, The Legal Aspects*, vol 1 (Harry Sacher Institute for Legislative Research and Comparative Law 1982) 13.

set committee in order to explain the legal situation in the territories taken by the IDF in that war.[97] Mr Shamgar mentioned both the Hague Regulations and GCIV. He explained that Israel had ratified GCIV in the nineteen-fifties and that while it had not ratified the Hague Convention, the provisions of the Hague Regulations bind every civilized nation. Mr Shamgar made no distinction between the various territories taken by Israel during the War.

During the first few months of the occupation the MAG's office took the application of the law of belligerent occupation in the West Bank seriously and gave legal advice accordingly. Thus, for example, in a letter written on behalf of the MAG dated 11 July 1967, a military lawyer wrote to the Officer Commanding the Central Command (which includes the West Bank) concerning his decision to seize land to be used as a firing zone. The lawyer stated that it is forbidden to establish a firing zone on land if there are local residents there or if the land is cultivated. He added that evicting persons from land in order to establish an area for military training is not allowed, from a political and moral point of view "as well as from grounds connected with international law." The lawyer cited article 49 of GCIV and stated that under this provision it is forbidden to forcibly remove civilians in occupied territory, save in the case when immediate military needs demand it.[98]

While initially the lawyers seemed to have no problem in regarding the territories taken in the War as occupied territories, politicians and senior foreign office officials were soon having difficulties with this categorization. In a secret memorandum dated 22 June 1967, Michael Comay, an adviser to

97 Minutes of Meeting 126 of the Knesset Constitution and Law Committee (5 July 1967).

98 The letter (in Hebrew) is available at <https://www.akevot.org.il/article/firing-zone-918-case-1967-legal-opinion-presented-high-court/> accessed 8 January 2025. The dramatic changes that have taken place in the way the authorities relate to the local inhabitants of the West Bank, and to Israel's commitment to international law is revealed in a case that reached the Supreme Court in this century. The military commander had declared land to be a 'firing zone' and ordered evictions of Palestinians living on the land in an area called Masafer Yatta. The Supreme Court upheld the eviction order and, ignoring the above letter that was submitted to the Court, held that article 49 does not apply to internal forcible removal of persons: HCJ 413/13 *Abu Aram v Minister of Defence* [4 May 2022]. For a devastating critique of the Court's judgment in this case see Orna Ben-Naftali and Eitan Diamond, 'No Place for Palestinians: The Israeli High Court of Justice Fades Out of the Global Community of Courts: The Farcical Tragedy of the 2022 Judgment on Masafer Yatta' (2023) 41 *Boston University International Law Journal* 47.

the Foreign Minister, expressed his opinion that all reference to "occupied" territories should be avoided.[99] Speaking in the Knesset a few days after Comay's memorandum, the Minister of Justice also refrained from referring to occupied territories and claimed that the legal outlook of the State of Israel is that the law, jurisdiction, and administration of the state applies to parts of the Land of Israel that are in actual fact in its sphere of sovereignty.[100]

3.3 *Non-Military Lawyers Step In*

Comay's memorandum obviously had no influence over Theodor Meron, at the time the young legal adviser in the Ministry of Foreign Affairs.[101] As pressure from Israelis to allow them to settle in the West Bank began to grow, Prime Minister Levy Eshkol asked for an opinion on the legality of settling Israeli citizens in the area. In a top secret memorandum written in September 1967, Meron opined that establishment of Israeli settlements in the area would be regarded as a violation of article 49(6) of GCIV.[102] At the same time, Meron wrote that "if it was decided on steps of Jewish settlement in the occupied territories, it seems to me that it is essential that the settlement be carried out by military and not civilian bodies. It is important, in my mind, that the settlement be in the framework of camps, that should outwardly have a temporary, not a permanent, character."[103] In this same opinion, Meron mentioned that Israeli officials were denying that the West

99 Comay's letter is available at <https://www.akevot.org.il/article/comay-memo-terminology/?full#popup/57adfcfad6f77d91a17433135ebed3ce> accessed 8 January 2025 [in Hebrew]. Comay was worried about the ICRC having a formal status in the newly occupied territories, rather than being allowed to operate there on what he termed a "pragmatic basis." He suggested that the territories be termed territories under military rule or "territories under Israel's control" and stated that he preferred the latter term.

100 Speech of Minister of Justice Shapira, 49 *Divrei Haknesset* 2420 (27 June 1967) [in Hebrew].

101 Meron later became Israel's ambassador in Canada. In 1977 he left the Israel foreign service and took up an appointment as a professor of international law at NYU. Meron subsequently became an American citizen and had a highly successful and impressive career as a law professor and as a judge and president of the International Tribunal for the Former Yugoslavia. He is regarded today as one of the foremost experts on international humanitarian law and international human rights law.

102 Israel State Archives, 153.8/7921/3A. Legal opinion, doc 289-291. Meron's opinion can be found at <https://haimwatzman.com/2008/09/kfar-etzion-the-meron-opinion-and-the-illegality-of-settlement/> accessed 8 January 2025.

103 ibid.

Bank is occupied territory, and claiming that the Armistice lines were only temporary military lines and not the political borders of the country that were no longer valid since Jordan had violated the Armistice Agreement. He pointed out that the government should be aware that international bodies did not accept that the territory was not occupied territory. Furthermore, he wrote that steps of Israel itself were not compatible with the claim that the territory was not occupied territory. As an example of such steps, Meron cited the reference in the first military order to GCIV.

It was not long before lawyers began to raise legal arguments in support of the view mentioned, and basically dismissed, by Meron. The first step in this direction was taken by Professor Yehuda Blum, at the time a young lecturer in international law at the Hebrew University and later Israel's UN representative. In 1968 Blum wrote an article in which he argued that since Jordan was an aggressor when it gained control over the West Bank in 1948, and that it had illegally annexed the West Bank in 1950, it had no sovereign rights in that territory when it was taken by Israel in 1967. Blum's conclusion was that the part of occupation law that applies to protection of the rights of the former sovereign should not apply in the West Bank. He added that since Israel had taken the territory in a war of self-defence, it had a better claim to the territory than Jordan. No mention was made of the right to self-determination of the Palestinian people living in the territory.[104]

Soon after Meron sent his memorandum to the Prime Minister, the provision in the military order mentioning GCIV was deleted and replaced by a provision that incorporated a specific provision of the Convention.[105] Whether this was done in response to Meron's memorandum or Blum's

104 Yehuda Z Blum, 'The Missing Reversioner: Reflections on the Status of Judea and Samaria' (1968) 3 *Israel Law Review* 279. In a later article Blum argued that Israel had never regarded its status in any area of the Land of Israel as that of an occupier: Yehuda Z Blum, 'The Redemption of Zion in International Law' (1971) 27 *Hapraklit* 315 [in Hebrew]. Blum's approach was challenged by Yoram Dinstein, 'Zion shall be Redeemed in International Law' (1971) 27 *Hapraklit* 5 [in Hebrew], and Yoram Dinstein, 'Zion was not Redeemed' or 'No Demonstrations but Deeds' (1972) 27 *Hapraklit* 519 [in Hebrew]. On Blum's seminal article see Eyal Benvenisti, 'An Article That Changed the Course of History' (2017) 50 *Israel Law Review* 269 and Yehuda Z Blum, 'The Status of Judea and Samaria Revisited: A Reply to Eyal Benvenisti' (2018) 51 *Israel Law Review* 165.

105 *Security Provisions Order (West Bank) (Amendment No 9) (Order No 144)*, 1967. The new provision incorporated the substance of art 69, GCIV (that relates to deduction of the period spent in pre-trial detention from the period of imprisonment) in the military orders. For details see Yaël Ronen, 'Blind in Their Own Cause: The

pending article is a matter for surmise.[106] Whatever the reason, the official position of the Government of Israel now became that it was doubtful whether GCIV applies to Israel's actions in the West Bank, although Israel would nevertheless abide by the humanitarian provisions in the Convention.[107] We shall consider the government's argument below.

The change in legal attitudes in order to cater to the policies of the Israeli government was not restricted to the change in the approach to application of GCIV. Quite soon after the occupation began, Minister of Defence Moshe Dayan adopted a policy of deporting Palestinians who were not cooperating with the military authorities to Jordan. When this policy came to the attention of Foreign Ministry Legal Adviser Meron, he realised that the policy was clearly incompatible with Article 49(1) of GCIV, which prohibits deportation of protected persons from occupied territory, "whatever the motive". In a memo to the Director General of the Ministry of Foreign Affairs, Meron expressed his objection to the deportations.[108] In his memo Meron mentioned that he had spoken to the MAG, Meir Shamgar, and that Shamgar agreed with his, Meron's, interpretation of Article 49(1). Meron wrote that Shamgar had informed him that he had explained his position to the relevant authorities, but that they had refused to abandon the policy.

Shamgar eventually became president of Israel's Supreme Court and in that capacity he headed the bench that heard a petition challenging the decision to deport Palestinians suspected of hostile activities.[109] The petitioners' main argument rested on Article 49(1) of GCIV. Despite the opinion that he had expressed as MAG, Shamgar wrote the judgment of the majority on the bench in which he rejected the argument that Article 49(1)

Military Courts in the West Bank' (2013) 2 *Cambridge Journal of International and Comparative Law* 738, 746.

106 In his autobiography, Meir Shamgar, who in September 1967 was still MAG and was about to be appointed Attorney General of Israel, refers to Blum's article and mentions that together with the denial by Israel's representatives to the UN that the territories were occupied, Blum's opinion formed the basis for the government's argument that GCIV did not apply to Israel's rule in the West Bank: Meir Shamgar, *An Autobiography* (Miskal—Yedioth Ahronoth and Chemed Books 2015) 107.

107 Meir Shamgar, 'The Observance of International Law in the Administered Territories' (1971) 1 *Israel Yearbook on Human Rights* 262.

108 Memorandum of T. Meron to Director General of Ministry of Foreign Affairs (20 December 1967) <https://www.akevot.org.il/article/deportation-policy-memo/#popup/f142e36c67703ed6318649fea7843451> [in Hebrew] accessed 20 January 2025.

109 HCJ 785/87 *'Abed Al-'Afou v IDF Commander in the West Bank* [1988] PD 42(3) 801.

recognizes no exceptions to the prohibition on deportation of protected persons and held that it does not apply to deportations of individuals on security grounds. His judgment, which was severely criticized,[110] did not enhance the Court's prestige.

A short time after the deletion of the reference to GCIV from the military order the Israeli Cabinet decided that official maps of Israel would not include the Green Line, namely the Armistice line that separated Israel from the West Bank from 1949 until 1967.[111] Since then maps of Israel show the whole territory of Mandatory Palestine, known to Israelis as the Land of Israel.[112]

3.4 Approach of the International Community

The first major UNSC resolution relating to the consequences of the June 1967 war was Resolution 242 of 22 November 1967.[113] This famous resolution, which is still regarded as the basis for a lasting peace between Israel and its neighbours,[114] does not mention the right of self-determination of the Palestinians. It does, however, mention the prohibition on the acquisition of territory by war and stipulates that a just and lasting peace must be based on two principles:

"(i) Withdrawal of Israeli forces from territory occupied in the recent conflict; and

---

110 Yoram Dinstein, 'Deportation from Occupied Territory' (1988) 13 *Tel Aviv University Law Review* 403; Kretzmer and Ronen (n 57) 424-430.

111 Resolution 9/b of Ministerial Committee on Foreign Affairs and Security (18 October 1967); Cabinet Committee on Security Resolution 21/b (12 November 1967). Both resolutions, which were marked as "top secret", are available at <https://www.akevot.org.il/article/ereasure-of-the-green-line/> [in Hebrew] accessed 8 January 2025. Soon after the above resolutions were passed the military commander promulgated a military order under which the term "Judea and Samaria" would, for every purpose, have the same meaning as the "area of the West Bank" (the term that had been used in military orders since June 1967): Order on Interpretation (Additional Provisions)(No. 3)(Order no. 187), 17 December 1967.

112 See the official map of Israel at <https://www.govmap.gov.il/?c=204000,595000&z=0&lang=en> accessed 8 January 2025.

113 UN Doc S/RES/242 (1967).

114 See, eg, UNSC Res 2334 (n 8) that reaffirms this and other Security Council resolutions on the Middle East.

(ii) Termination of all claims or states of belligerency and respect for and acknowledgment of the sovereignty, territorial integrity and political independence of every State in the area and their right to live in peace within secure and recognized borders free from acts or threats of force."[115]

Since that Resolution was passed the UNSC has referred on numerous occasions to the status of the West Bank as occupied territory in which GCIV applies.[116] This has been the consistent view of the UN General Assembly, the ICRC and many states. It is also the view of the International Court of Justice.[117] The Supreme Court of Israel has also held that Israel governs the West Bank under a regime of belligerent occupation.[118]

Given this consistent and virtually unanimous view of the international community on the status of the West Bank as occupied territory it is important to consider the legal arguments that have been raised by lawyers challenging this view. I now turn to a critical analysis of these arguments.

---

115 A significant difference between the English and French texts of the Resolution has led to a difference of opinion on the scope of the demand that Israel withdraw from territory occupied in the June 1967 War. While the English text refers to "territory occupied", the French text refers to "des territoires occupés." Relying on the English text, Israel may argue that by withdrawing from the Sinai Peninsula it has withdrawn from territory occupied in the conflict and has therefore complied with the Resolution. Relying on the French (and also the Spanish) version of the Resolution, the counter argument is that Israel has to withdraw from all the territory occupied in 1967. On the background to the text of Resolution 242 see David McDowall 'Clarity or ambiguity? The withdrawal clause of UN Security Council Resolution 242' (2014) 90 *International Affairs* (Royal Institute of International Affairs) 1367. For presentation of Israel's understanding of the Resolution see Ruth Lapidoth, 'The Misleading Interpretation of UN Security Council Resolution 242 (1967)' (2011) 23 *Jewish Political Studies Review* 7. For differing views on the interpretation of the Resolution see, eg, Winston P. Nagan and Aitza M. Haddad, 'Recognition of Palestinian Statehood: A Clarification of the Interests of the Concerned Parties' (2012) 40 *Georgia Journal of Int'l and Comp. L* 341, (arguing that Israel's settlement activity flies in the face of Resolution 242 and is therefore unlawful); John McHugo, 'Resolution 242: A Legal Reappraisal of the Right Wing Israeli Interpretation of the Withdrawal Phrase With Reference to the Conflict Between Israel and the Palestinians' (2002) 51 *Int'l and Comp L Quarterly 851* (arguing that the Resolution requires Israeli withdrawal from all the territories taken in 1967); Eugene Kontorovic, 'Resolution 242 Revisited: New Evidence on the Required Scope of Israeli Withdrawal' (2015) *16 Chi J of Int'l L.* 127 (arguing that the Resolution only requires partial Israeli withdrawal from territories taken in 1967).

116 See UNSC Res 2334 (n 8) and the Security Council resolutions mentioned therein.

117 *Wall* Advisory Opinion (n 82).

118 See ch 6.

Chapter 4: Arguments Challenging the Status of the West Bank as Occupied Territory

4.1 Non-Application of Fourth Geneva Convention

As we saw above, a provision in the first military order issued in the West Bank in June 1967 stated that the military courts that had been established to try persons accused of security offences must abide by the provisions of GCIV. We also saw that a few months after the occupation began this provision was deleted from the military order. Deletion of the reference to GCIV followed objections of politicians and public officials to the view that the territory taken in 1967 was occupied territory, and the legal argument of an academic lawyer rejecting the characterisation of the West Bank as territory to which the whole corpus of the law of belligerent occupation applies.[119]

The government's argument on non-application of GCIV was presented by Attorney General Meir Shamgar.[120] The argument is based on article 2 of GCIV that states:

> In addition to the provisions which shall be implemented in peace-time, the present Convention shall apply to all cases of declared war or of any other armed conflict which may arise between two or more of the High Contracting Parties, even if the state of war is not recognized by one of them.
>
> The Convention shall also apply to all cases of partial or total occupation of the territory of a High Contracting Party, even if the said occupation meets with no armed resistance.

Relying on the second paragraph the government argument is that since the West Bank was occupied by Jordan in 1949 and was not the sovereign territory of a "High Contracting Party" when it was occupied by Israel in 1967, the Convention does not formally apply to Israel's control over this territory.[121]

119 Blum, 'The Missing Reversioner' (n 104).

120 Shamgar (n 107).

121 Egypt never claimed sovereignty over Gaza. Jordan annexed the West Bank in 1950, but the argument is that this annexation was unlawful, and was only recognized

This argument has been rejected by the ICRC,[122] leading Israeli academics,[123] experts in international law,[124] states Parties to GCIV,[125] the UN Security Council[126] and the International Court of Justice.[127] The drafting history of Article 2 reveals that the second paragraph was introduced in order to ensure application of the Convention in cases of occupation that did not result from armed conflict.[128] This was thought necessary as a result of the Nazi occupation of Denmark, which did not initially meet with armed resistance.[129] The second paragraph is irrelevant in cases of occupation arising from armed conflict, since these are covered by the first paragraph.[130] According to the first paragraph, the Convention applies to

---

by two states, UK and Pakistan. The argument relating to the illegality on use of force by Jordan when it invaded Palestine in May 1948 is fully presented by Blum, 'The Missing Reversioner' (n 104). The West Bank had never been part of Jordan's territory, and Jordan was an aggressor when it invaded Palestine in order to frustrate implementation of the UN Partition Plan. After taking control over the area through use of force, Jordan became on occupying power in the territory. Hence its annexation of the territory, which was condemned by the Arab League, had no effect in international law. In a case before the Supreme Court in 1972 (HCJ 256/72 *Electricity Corporation of Jerusalem District v Minister of Defence* [1972] PD 27(1) 124 (hereinafter: *Electricity Co (No 1)*) the government submitted a certificate from the Director General of the Ministry of Foreign Affairs that between 1948-1967 Israel regarded the West Bank as occupied territory.

122 Peter Maurer, 'Challenges to International Humanitarian Law: Israel's Occupation Policy' (2012) 94 *International Review of the Red Cross* 1503.

123 Yoram Dinstein, 'The International Law of Belligerent Occupation and Human Rights,' (1978) 8 *Israel Yearbook on Human Rights* 104, 107; Benvenisti (n 1) 207.

124 eg Stephen M Boyd, 'The Applicability of International Law to the Occupied Territories' (1971) 1 *Israel Yearbook on Human Rights* 258; Adam Roberts, 'What is a military occupation?' (1984) 54 *British Yearbook of International Law* 249, 281-283; Hans Peter Gesser, 'Protection of the Civilian Population' in Dieter Fleck (ed), *The Handbook of Humanitarian Law in Armed Conflicts* (OUP 1995) 209, 244.

125 'Declaration from the Conference of High Contracting Parties to the Fourth Geneva Convention', 4 Dec 2001, cited in: *In a Dark Hour: The Use of Civilians during IDF Arrest Operations* (Human Rights Watch, April 2002) <https://www.hrw.org/reports/2002/israel2/index.htm#TopOfPage> accessed 8 January 2025.

126 eg UNSC Res 446 (n 8).

127 *Wall* Advisory Opinion (n 82).

128 International Committee of the Red Cross, *Report on the Work of the Conference of Government Experts for the Study of the Conventions for the Protection of War Victims* (ICRC 1947); International Committee of the Red Cross, *Commentary on IV Geneva Convention Relative to the Protection of Civilian Persons in Time of War* (Jean S Pictet (ed), ICRC 1958) (hereinafter: *ICRC Commentary*).

129 Dieter Schindler, 'The different types of armed conflicts according to the Geneva Conventions and Protocols' (1979) II *Recueil des Cours* 121, 132.

130 ICRC Commentary (n 128); Roberts (n 124).

territory occupied in the 1967 armed conflict between Israel and Jordan, which were both parties to the Convention at the time of the conflict (and have remained so since).[131]

GCIV is not concerned with the sovereignty of parties to a conflict. Rather, it applies to all cases in which territory is occupied in the course of an armed conflict, irrespective of the status of that territory.[132] The object of GCIV is to protect civilians, and not the political interests of the parties to an armed conflict. Hence it makes little sense to argue that the Convention does not apply when the sovereignty over the occupied territory is disputed. As the recent ICRC Commentary on the First Geneva Convention explains, adopting the Israeli interpretation would mean that any occupying power could avoid application of GCIV simply by disputing the sovereign status of the state that held the territory before it was occupied.[133] Furthermore, as mentioned above, in the article in which he raised the argument that the West Bank did not belong to a sovereign state when occupied by Israel in 1967, Yehuda Blum stated categorically that the humanitarian obligations of the occupying power do apply in this situation.[134] The object of GCIV was to codify these obligations.

In the changing attitudes to the application of GCIV we see quite clearly how the political interests of the occupying power influenced the position adopted by the lawyers. When drawing up the military orders that would be promulgated in the case of a war with the neighbouring countries, and in his appearance before the Knesset Committee one month after the 1967 War ended, Meir Shamgar, then the MAG, assumed quite correctly that GCIV would apply to any territory occupied during the war. Only later, when he became Attorney General of the State, and was exposed to the evolving political interests in the West Bank, did he modify his stand and advance the above interpretation.

Over and above his formal argument, based on the interpretation of article 2 of the Convention, Shamgar's substantive argument was that rec-

131 *Wall* Advisory Opinion (n 82).

132 'Note of Red Cross' quoted in (1977) 7 *Israel Yearbook on Human Rights* 169-70; Shamgar (n 96) 32.

133 ICRC, *Commentary on First Geneva Convention 1949* (2016) para 323-327. See also *Eritrea-Ethiopia Claims Commission, Partial Award: Central Front - Ethiopia's Claim 2* (28 April 2004) para 29. Referring to both the Hague Regulations and GCIV the Commission stated that "neither text suggests that only territory the title to which is clear and uncontested can be occupied territory."

134 Blum, 'The Missing Reversioner' (n 104).

ognizing formal application of the Convention would imply recognition of Jordan's status in the area prior to the 1967 War.[135] This argument is rather puzzling. If the government were really concerned lest it recognize Jordan's sovereignty over the West Bank, it should have raised objections to application of the Hague Regulations, since Article 43 of those Regulations refers to the "legitimate authority in the occupied territory having passed into the hands of the occupant...". GCIV contains no such reference. It is a purely humanitarian convention that aims to ensure protection of civilians without room for any political judgment or considerations. The States Parties undertake to respect and ensure respect for the Convention "in all circumstances" (Article 1). Yet as we shall see below, while Shamgar did indeed refer to application of the whole of the law of belligerent occupation, government lawyers have never seriously argued that the Hague Regulations do not apply to Israel's actions in the West Bank.[136] In fact they rely on them consistently in their arguments before the Supreme Court. It seems then that the real reasons for withdrawing from the recognition of the formal application of GCIV in the West Bank had nothing to do with the legal implications vis-a-vis Jordan's status in the West Bank. We must therefore seek the explanation somewhere else.

A number of possibilities arise. It was clear to decision-makers in Israel's Ministry of Foreign Affairs that many of the measures of the military in the newly occupied territories were incompatible with provisions in GCIV.[137] Rather than calling for a halt in use of such measures the decision-makers

---

135 Shamgar (n 96) 42.

136 In HCJ 1661/05 *Gaza Coast Regional Council v The Knesset* [2005] PD 59(2) 481, para 4, the Supreme Court declared: "There was never any disagreement over the application of the Hague Regulations on the Laws and Customs of War on Land, 1907 in Judea and Samaria.."

137 In March 1968 senior officials in the Ministry of Foreign affairs cabled Israel's UN mission explaining why Israel does not formally recognize the applicability of GCIV to the situation on the West Bank: that recognition of the formal application of the Convention "will emphasize difficult problems vis a vis the Convention as regards blowing up houses, deportations, settlement and more". This explanation is available at <https://akevot.org.il/article/ny-meron-cable/#popup/1b8571513de641067a2710a99a23b1f9> [in Hebrew] accessed 13 January 2025. Also see the document of the Foreign Ministry prepared in preparation for the visit of a senior official of the ICRC, in which they described Israeli practices which were regarded as incompatible with GCIV: <https://www.akevot.org.il/article/umbricht-brief/#popup/efed0e1b0f83312a2b8ec3f66a83c3e0> [in Hebrew] accessed 13 January 2025.

preferred to contest application of the Convention.[138] Another possibility is related to Theodor Meron's opinion concerning the illegality under GCIV of establishing Israeli settlements in the West Bank. As the government was determined to go ahead with settlements it saw fit to contest the Convention's application. This explanation would seem to find support in the government's statement that the IDF would comply with the humanitarian provisions of the Convention. This statement rests on the dubious grounds that establishment of Israeli settlements in the area has no effect on the rights of the Palestinian inhabitants of the area.

To summarize: the Government of Israel has stuck to its original position, presented by AG Meir Shamgar, that GCIV does not formally apply in the West Bank, but that as a matter of policy the military authorities would comply with its humanitarian provisions. This view is not well-founded and has found no support in the international community.

4.2 The West Bank Was Not Part of the Sovereign Territory of another State

The argument against application of the Geneva Convention in the specific situation of the West Bank, rests, as we have seen, on an interpretation of the text of the Convention. Government lawyers continue to rely on the Hague Regulations in defending the actions of the military commander in the West Bank before the Supreme Court of Israel, and that court has held time and again that as part of customary law, these Regulations bind the military authorities in the West Bank. Nevertheless, in international fora and in the domestic political arena the government continues to argue that Israel is not an occupying power, and that therefore the Hague Regulations do not apply *de jure*.[139] According to this argument, reflected in a letter of

138 In early July, 1967 Minister of Defence Moshe Dayan reported to the Cabinet that together with the deputy director general of the Ministry of Foreign Affairs, he had met with a representative of the International Committee of the Red Cross (ICRC), who had spoken of Israel's duty to comply with GCIV. Dayan told the Cabinet that he was not familiar with the Convention, but that the deputy director general had told him that it was "a load of trouble" and that Israel should not even consider "accepting it". Dayan told the ICRC representative that the legal advisers were examining the situation and that in the meantime Israel would be prepared to discuss specific issues without accepting that the Convention applies. Minutes of Cabinet Meeting 55/5727 (2 July 1967) 14-15.

139 See *Request for an Order Requiring an Article 18(1) Notice* (2024) ICC-01/18-355, ICC Pre-Trial Chamber I, <https://www.icc-cpi.int/sites/default/files/Related

the Cabinet Secretary dated 19 June 2023, the government has agreed to comply with the Hague Regulations as a matter of policy, although legally they do not apply to the State's actions in the West Bank.[140]

Originally raised by Yehuda Blum[141] and subsequently by Eugene Rostow,[142] the crux of this argument is that only territory of another state can become occupied territory. Since Jordan had illegally annexed the West Bank in 1950, it was not the sovereign power of the territory when it was taken by the IDF in 1967. Neither did any other state have sovereignty over the territory. Support for this argument may be found in the heading to section III of the Hague Regulations that refers to "Military Authority over the Territory of the Hostile **State**".

I have already considered this argument as far as it relates to the interpretation of GCIV. In this part I shall briefly refer to the wider argument that only territory that was the sovereign territory of another state becomes occupied territory when a hostile army gains control over the territory in the course of an armed conflict.

In an era in which the only actors recognized by international law were states and international organs, while peoples and individuals had no standing, it was possible to restrict the concept of occupation to territory of one state that had been occupied by another. However, international law does not remain static and this position of international law is no longer valid.

Article 1 of the UN Charter states expressly that one of the Organization's purposes is "(t)o develop friendly relations among nations based on respect for the principle of equal rights and self-determination of peoples." Article 1 common to the International Covenant on Economic, Social and Cultural Rights, 1966 and to the International Covenant on Civil and Political

---

Records/0902ebd180994069.pdf> accessed 13 January 2025, para 116: "Israel is administering territory with respect to which sovereignty is in abeyance. This does not diminish Israel's obligations to administer the territory in accordance with international law, as it has undertaken to do, notwithstanding its position regarding the inapplicability of the law of occupation *de jure* under these unique circumstances."

140 Letter dated 19.6.2023 of Yossi Fuchs, Cabinet Secretary (on file with author) (hereinafter: Letter 19.6.2023).

141 While Blum only contested application of part of the law of belligerent occupation, his article (n 104) provided the basis for the wider argument that the law of belligerent occupation does not apply in the West Bank.

142 Eugene V Rostow, 'Palestinian Self-Determination: Possible Futures for the Unallocated Territories of the Palestine Mandate' (1979) 5 *Yale Studies in World Public Order* 147.

Rights, 1966 declares that "All peoples have the right of self-determination." The ICJ has made it clear that in interpreting the mandates of the League of Nations and other international instruments of the time later developments in international law must be taken into account. These include the right of self-determination of peoples.[143]

In ignoring these principles both Blum and Rostow were adopting attitudes that were unfortunately prevalent in the 19th Century and the early part of the 20th Century. As Lieblich and Benvenisti explain in their book on the law of belligerent occupation, until the 20th Century international law was entirely Eurocentric. The prevailing view was that the law of belligerent occupation only applied in Europe, and not to the territories inhabited by what were termed "uncivilized peoples" who were not capable, in European eyes, of governing themselves.[144] Lieblich and Benvenisti write:

> In this sense, like most laws of war of the time, the law of occupation served some humanitarian purposes, but was also a colonial marker of distinction between subjects and nonsubjects of international law. Only in the 20th century, with the advent of the principles of sovereign equality and self-determination, did international law cease to make that distinction formally. **These principles now require that the law of occupation apply to the territories of all states or peoples.**[145]

The denial that territory that was not part of the sovereign territory of another state cannot be regarded as occupied territory was based, inter

---

143 *Legal Consequences for States of the Continued Presence of South Africa in Namibia (South West Africa) notwithstanding Security Council Resolution 276* (Advisory Opinion) [1970] ICJ Rep 16 (hereinafter: *Namibia* Advisory Opinion), para 53: "viewing the institutions of 1919, the Court must take into consideration the changes which have occurred in the supervening half-century, and its interpretation cannot remain unaffected by the subsequent development of law, through the Charter of the United Nations and by way of customary law. Moreover, an international instrument has to be interpreted and applied within the framework of the entire legal system prevailing at the time of the interpretation. In the domain to which the present proceedings relate, the last fifty years, as indicated above, have brought important developments. These developments leave little doubt that the ultimate objective of the sacred trust was the self-determination and independence of the peoples concerned".

144 Samuel Moyn, *Humane: How the United States Abandoned Peace and Reinvented War 91-97* (Farrar, Straus and Giroux 2021). The most extreme expression of this view is presented in Elbridge Colby, 'How to Fight Savage Tribes' (1927) 21 *American Journal of International Law* 279.

145 Lieblich and Benvenisti (n 1) 46 (emphasis added).

alia, on denial of the right of the Palestinians to self-determination.[146] Rostow admitted that he regarded the notion of self-determination of peoples as problematical, absent any definition of the term "peoples." It must be stressed that in the present context it is not essential to recognize the Palestinians as a people in order to reach the conclusion that the inhabitants of the West Bank and Gaza are entitled to self-determination.[147] As the ICJ held in the *Chagos* case, the right of self-determination of the *population* of a territory that was subject to foreign rule was established in the nineteen-sixties.[148] Of course, now that the Palestinians have gained universal recognition as a people, the Rostow-Blum view becomes even more problematical.

Blum's failure to relate to the rights of the Palestinians in the West Bank is inexplicable. In his original article Blum dismissed the idea that the West Bank could have become *terra nullius* when the Mandate ended, as this would have implied that it was up for grabs by any state. Blum explained that there were six theories regarding the question of sovereignty of territory subject to a League of Nations mandate. One of these was that the inhabitants of the territory are the sovereign.[149] For reasons which he failed to present, in discussing the issue of sovereignty after the Mandate ended Blum did not consider the implications of this theory. Rather he confined the issue to competing claims of two states, neither of which could have claimed to be the sovereign when the Mandate ended. In other words, if, as Blum admitted, the West Bank was not *terra nullius* when Israel entered

---

146 Rostow (n 142) 153: "Despite its great political appeal, the idea of "self-determination" for all "peoples" is a puzzling and complex factor in the political life of an international system based on the existence and sanctity of states."

147 See Allan Gerson, 'Trustee-occupant: the legal status of Israel's presence in the West Bank' (1973) 14 *Harvard Journal of International Law* 1, 43.

148 *Legal Consequences of the Separation of the Chagos Archipelago from Mauritius in 1965* (Advisory Opinion) [2019] ICJ Rep 95, paras 144-162. The Court stated that "the legal régime of non self-governing territories, as set out in Chapter XI of the Charter, was based on the progressive development of their institutions so as to lead the **populations** concerned to exercise their right to self-determination." (ibid para 147, emphasis added).

149 Blum, 'The Missing Reverioner' (n 104). In presenting the various theories regarding sovereignty over mandate territory Blum relied on RN Chowdhuri, *Supranational Mandates and Trusteeship Systems: A Comparative Study* (Martinus Nijhoff 1955). Blum ignored the fact that Chowdhuri took the view that as long as the mandate continued sovereignty over the territory was in abeyance, but that when the mandate ended sovereignty was vested automatically in the people of the territory: ibid. 236.

the area in June 1967, the sovereignty must have been somewhere. The only possible answer is that it belonged to the inhabitants of the territory.

In summary: in the post WWII world there is no basis for the view that only the territory of a sovereign state can be subject to belligerent occupation. All populations have the right not to be dominated by a "hostile army". Hence, even if we accept that the West Bank and Gaza were not the sovereign territory of another state when occupied by the IDF in 1967, those territories were not part of Israel's sovereign territory, and from the point of view of their populations, the IDF was clearly a "hostile army." Hence once placed under the authority of that army they became occupied territory.[150]

The government's argument that it only applies the Hague Regulations as a matter of policy, although they do not apply *de jure*, is problematical from another point of view. As mentioned above, government lawyers who defend the actions of the military commander in the West Bank before the Supreme Court of Israel regularly rely on the Hague Regulations. In one major case concerning seizure of private land that we discuss below, the Court explained that the only source of power of the military commander to seize the property was the international law of belligerent occupation. If that body of law did not apply the military commander had acted *ultra vires*.[151] This explanation is relevant in regard to hundreds of acts performed by the military commander since June 1967. Denying that the Hague Regulations do not apply *de jure* means that in all these years the military commander has been exceeding his legal powers and that many of his acts were invalid.

150 See Article 42 of the Hague Regulations, 1907: "Territory is considered occupied when it is actually placed under the authority of the hostile army."

151 HCJ 390/79 *Azat Muhammad Mustafa Dweikat v Government of Israel* [1979] PD 34(1) 1 (hereinafter: *Elon Moreh* case).

Chapter 5: Effect of the British Mandate on the Status of the West Bank

5.1 Introduction

In a series of articles, Professor Eugene Rostow, a law professor, former dean of Yale Law School and senior official in the U.S. State department during the Johnson Administration, challenged the designation of the West Bank and Gaza Strip as occupied territory. He first raised his claim in an article published in 1979[152] and refined it in subsequent articles[153] and a "Correspondence" with the Editor-in-Chief of the American Journal of International Law.[154] Rostow based his claim that these territories are not occupied on two arguments. First, that the League of Nations Mandate over Palestine continues to apply in those parts of Palestine that had not become part of either Israel or Jordan; and secondly, as we saw above, that only territory that is the sovereign territory of another state becomes occupied territory when taken in war. Rostow argued that the right of Jews to settle in Palestine, which in his mind had been guaranteed in the Mandate, continues to apply in the West Bank and Gaza Strip. He refused to regard the Arab inhabitants of the West Bank and Gaza as a people entitled to self-determination. Alongside his reservations over the definition of "peoples", Rostow argued that recognition of the right of the Arab inhabitants of Palestine to self-determination was rejected by the international community when

152 See Rostow (n 142).

153 Eugene V Rostow, 'Israel's Settlement Rights are Unassailable' *New York Times* (19 September 1983); Eugene V Rostow, 'A False Start in the Middle East', *Commentary* (October 1989).

154 'Correspondence' (1990) 84 *American Journal of International Law* 717. This Correspondence was written in response to the article of Adam Roberts, 'Prolonged Military Occupation: The Israeli-Occupied Territories Since 1967' (1990) 84 *American Journal of International Law* 44. Robert's article was a revised version of a paper he presented at a conference organized in Jerusalem in 1988 by the Palestinian NGO, Al-Haq. The papers presented at this conference were published in Emma Playfair (ed), *International Law and the Administration of Occupied Territories: Two Decades of the Israeli Occupation of the West Bank and Gaza Strip* (OUP 1990).

it granted the Mandate to Great Britain and instructed Great Britain to facilitate creation of a home for the Jewish people in Palestine.[155]

Rostow's argument was taken up by others,[156] and was adopted by a committee established by the government in 2012 to write a report on regulating settlements in the West Bank.[157] But, perhaps most importantly, it was adopted by the present government in its attempts to dispute the status of the West Bank as occupied territory. Soon after the present government that was formed in December 2022 had committed itself to "regularizing" all outposts established in the West Bank without formal government approval, an attorney acting on behalf of Adalah, an Israeli NGO, wrote to the government complaining that implementation of that commitment involved violation of the law of belligerent occupation. In his reply to the letter, dated 19 June 2023, the Cabinet secretary challenged the view that the West Bank is occupied territory.[158] Relying on both of Rostow's arguments the Cabinet Secretary stated that there is no legal impediment to establishment of Israeli settlements in the area. In his view Israel applies the law of belligerent occupation as a matter of policy, although that law does not apply *de jure*. While not mentioning the grounds for the argument raised by Rostow, in a memorandum relating to the jurisdiction of the ICC over the situation in Palestine, the Attorney General of Israel also stated that the law of belligerent occupation does not apply *de jure* in the West Bank.[159] Finally,

---

155 Rostow (n 142).

156 Talia Einhorn, *The Status of Judea & Samaria (the West Bank) and Gaza and the Settlements in International Law* (Jerusalem Center for Public Affairs 14 August 2014) <https://jcpa.org/article/status-of-settlements-in-international-law/> accessed 13 January 2025.

157 The Levy Report (in Hebrew) is available at <https://www.gov.il/BlobFolder/news/spokeedmond090712/he/documents_doch090712.pdf> accessed 13 January 2025. For incisive criticism of the report see Orna Ben-Naftali and Rafi Reznik, 'The Astro-Nomos: On International Legal Paradigms and the Legal Status of the West Bank' (2015) 14 *Washington University Global Studies Law Review* 399; Yesh Din, *Unprecedented: A Legal Analysis of the Report of the Committee to Examine the Status of Building in Judea and Samaria [the West Bank] ("The Levy Committee") –International and Administrative Aspects* (2014). <http://files.yesh-din.org/userfiles/file/Reports-English/Yesh%20Din%20-%20Chasar%20Takdim%20English%20-%20Web-%2016_6.pdf> accessed 13 January 2025; Nathaniel Berman, 'San Remo in Shilo: The settlements and legal history' *The Times Of Israel* (19 July 2012) <https://blogs.timesofisrael.com/san-remo-in-shilo-the-settlements-and-legal-history/> accessed 13 January 2025.

158 See Letter of 19.6.2023 (n 140).

159 State of Israel, Office of the Attorney General, *The International Criminal Court's Lack of Jurisdiction over the So-Called "Situation in Palestine"* (20 December 2019)

after the International Court of Justice delivered its Advisory Opinion on the Legal Consequences arising from Israel's policies and practices in the occupied Palestinian territory, PM Netanyahu responded by presenting the Cabinet with an opinion by an Israeli academic who still hangs onto the Rostow argument of the Jews' right to the land under the League of Nations mandate.[160]

Rostow's argument has received no traction in the international community, as witnessed by numerous resolutions of the UN Security Council[161] and the UN General Assembly,[162] alongside two Advisory Opinions of the ICJ.[163] All these organs of the UN are of the opinion that the West Bank is occupied territory, and that by establishing settlements for its citizens there, Israel has violated its international obligations as an occupying power. This is also the opinion of most states and the International Committee of the Red Cross.[164] The Supreme Court of Israel has also held that the West Bank is subject to a regime of belligerent occupation.[165] Nevertheless, given the centrality of Rostow's arguments in the approach of the Government of Israel towards the legal status of the West Bank, and the legality of its

---

24 <https://www.gov.il/en/pages/20-12-2019> accessed 13 January 2025. This argument was repeated in a brief submitted to the International Criminal Court, challenging that Court's jurisdiction over Israel's actions in the Occupied Territories: *Request for an Order Requiring an Article 18(1) Notice* (2024) ICC-01/18-355 (n 139).

160 See Chen Ma'anit, 'Netanyahu presented the government with a draft resolution rejecting the Hague Advisory Opinion, that was written without the cooperation of the Attorney General' *Ha'aretz* (21 July 2024) <https://www.haaretz.co.il/news/politi/2024-07-21/ty-article/.premium/00000190-d4e5-dbb4-a7d2-dfefdc370000>. The view of the academic lawyer who wrote the opinion is presented in Einhorn (n 156).

161 For example see: UNSC. Res. 465 (n 8); UNSC Res 446 (n 8); UNSC Res 452 (22 July 1979) UN Doc S/RES/452(1979); UNSC Res 2334 (n 8).

162 For example see: UNGA Res 2546 (11 December 1969) UN Doc A/RES/2546; UNGA Res 3414 (5 December 1975) UN Doc A/RES/3414; UNGA Res 31/61 (9 December 1976) UN Doc A/RES/31/61; UNGA Res 77/126 (12 December 2022) UN Doc A/RES/77/126; UNGA Res 12626 (18 September 2024) UN Doc A/RES/12626.

163 *Wall* Advisory Opinion (n 82); Advisory Opinion, *Occupied Palestinian Territory* (n 9).

164 Matthias Lanz, Emilie Max and Oliver Hoehne, 'The Conference of the High Contracting Parties to the Geneva Conventions of 17 December 2014 and the Duty to Ensure Respect for International Humanitarian Law' (2014) 96 *International Review of the Red Cross* 1115; Maurer (n 122) 1506.

165 *Elon Moreh* case (n 151); HCJ 393/82 *Jami'yat Iskan v IDF Commander in Judaea and Samaria* [1983] PD 37(4) 785; *Gaza Coast* case (n 136); HCJ 2164/09 *Yesh Din – Volunteers for Human Rights v the Commander of the IDF Forces in the West Bank* (12 December 2011)(hereinafter: *Yesh Din (Quarries)* case).

settlement policy there, it is important to subject Rostow's arguments to a critical analysis. In order to do so we must examine the background and legal basis of the British Mandate over Palestine. Before doing so I see fit to mention that at the time of the Mandate and ever since there have been scholars and political figures who have argued that the Mandate was illegal,[166] and even that it was never valid.[167] For the purposes of the present discussion, it is not important to review these arguments, since if the Mandate was never valid, Rostow's arguments must be dismissed out of hand. I rest the following discussion of the Mandate on the widely accepted view, expressed by James Crawford in his book on creation of states in international law, that the arguments against the validity of the Mandate must be rejected.[168]

166 For presentation of the arguments against the validity of the Mandate, see Kattan (n 15) 54-63; 117-145; John Strawson, *Partitioning Palestine: Legal Fundamentalism in the Palestinian-Israeli Conflict* (Pluto Press 2010) 66-70. For an early Palestinian argument against the Mandate see W.F. Boustany, *The Palestine Mandate: Invalid and Impracticable* (Beirut 1936).

167 John Quigley, *Britain and its Mandate over Palestine: Legal Chicanery on a World Stage* (Anthem Press 2022). Quigley argues that the League of Nations was not authorised to grant a mandate over territory that was part of the Ottoman Empire before Turkey had renounced its sovereignty over the territory. As the Treaty of Sevres was never ratified, Turkey had not renounced its sovereignty when the League Council approved the Mandate in July 1922, nor when it decided that the Mandate would enter into force in September 1923. But in August 2023 Turkey ratified the Lausanne Treaty, in which it renounced its sovereignty over all territories beyond the borders of Turkey recognized in the Treaty, "the future of these territories... being settled or to be settled by the parties concerned." *Treaty of peace with Turkey Signed at Lausanne* (24 July 1923) 28 *League of Nations Treaty Series* 11, art 16.

168 See Crawford (n 49) 428-430.

5.2 Background to the Mandate System[169]

As the First World War neared its end, the imperial powers Britain and France reached an agreement to divide the Middle Eastern territories of the Ottoman Empire between themselves.[170] The US president, Woodrow Wilson, was horrified when he learned of this agreement.[171] The 14 points to guide the post-War peace arrangements that Wilson presented to Congress in January 1918 included the principle that in determining the fate of territories that had been part of the defeated empires "the interests of the populations concerned must have equal weight with the equitable claims of the government whose title is to be determined."[172] This principle is regarded as the first expression of the idea that in determining the sovereignty over territory that had been part of a colonial empire, self-determination of the people living there should be a guiding political principle.[173]

---

169 For a detailed description of the background to the Mandate system, see Susan Pedersen, *The Guardians: The League of Nations and the Crisis of Empire* (OUP 2015) 17-44. For earlier discussions of this system see J Stoyanovsky, *The Mandate for Palestine* (Longmans 1928); Norman Bentwich, *The Mandates System* (Longmans 1930); Quincy Wright, *Mandates Under the League of Nations* (University of Chicago Press 1930). Also see Malcolm Shaw, 'The League of Nations Mandate System and the Palestine Mandate: What Did and Does It Say about International Law and What Did and Does It Say about Palestine' (2016) 49 *Israel Law Review* 287.

170 On this agreement, known as the Sykes-Picot agreement, see James Barr, *A Line in the Sand: The Anglo-French Struggle for the Middle East, 1914–1948*, (2012); Margaret Macmillan, *Paris 1919: Six Months that Changed the World* (2001) 382-388; Schneer (n 12) 76-86, 220-236; Charles D Smith, *Palestine and the Arab-Israeli Conflict: A History with Documents* (7th edn, Bedford/St. Martin's 2010) 63-66; Marina Ottaway, *Learning from Sykes-Picot* (Wilson Center, Middle East Program, Occasional Paper Series Fall 2015) <https://www.wilsoncenter.org/sites/default/files/media/documents/publication/learning_from_sykes_picot.pdf> accessed 13 January 2025.

171 The agreement remained secret until it was revealed by the Russian leaders after the Russian revolution. When Wilson learned of the Agreement he declared that he was not going to give in to "little groups of ambitious men who were accustomed to use their fellow men as pawns and tools" (cited by James Barr (n 170) 2).

172 Wilson's 14 points may be found on the site of the US Library of Congress <https://www.loc.gov/collections/world-war-i-rotogravures/articles-and-essays/events-and-statistics/wilsons-fourteen-points/> accessed 13 January 2025.

173 Derek Heater, *National Self-Determination: Woodrow Wilson and His Legacy* (Palgrave Macmillan 1994); Allen Lynch, 'Woodrow Wilson and the principle of 'national self-determination': a reconsideration' (2002) 28 *Review of International Studies* 419; Daniel Thürer and Thomas Burri, 'Self-Determination' in *Max Planck Encyclopedia of Public International Law IX* 113 (2012).

There was a clear clash between the colonial aspirations of Britain and France and Wilson's principle. The Mandate System was devised as a compromise between the two imperial powers and the US.[174] Hence, the Mandate System emerged out of the "potent brew of liberal internationalism, imperial humanitarianism, and sheer territorial acquisitiveness."[175]

It is important to appreciate the colonial background of the Mandate system for two reasons. Firstly, it should be considered when interpreting Article 22 of the League of Nations Covenant that laid the legal foundation for the Mandate system. Secondly, it is highly relevant when attempts are made to base rights on this system in the twentieth-first century, in which international law has rejected colonialism.

---

174 South Africa's Prime Minister, Jan Smuts, played a decisive role in devising the Mandate System: Pedersen (n 169) 27; Mark Mazower, *No Enchanted Palace: The End of Empire and the Ideological Origins of the United Nations* (Princeton University Press 2009) §§ 418 in digital edition. Smuts presented his idea in a small booklet: JC Smuts, *The League of Nations: A Practical Suggestion* (London Hodder and Stoughton 1918), in which he wrote that the League of Nations policy must be based on "no annexation and self-determination of nations." Mazower writes that Smuts regarded his proposal as a small gesture of Britain towards the U.S that paved the way for Britain to retain its empire. Smuts, the South African racist, was convinced that the white man had the task of protecting civilization in Africa. He favoured "imperial internationalism" based on the importance of protecting the existence of the British Empire (see Caroline Elkins, *Legacy of Violence: A History of the British Empire* (Knopf 2022) paras 128-130). According to his racist outlook, Smuts believed that his proposal was appropriate for countries that had been part of the Russian, Austro-Hungarian and Ottoman Empires, but not those of the German Empire, since they were in Africa and the Pacific Islands that were inhabited by "barbarians" who could not rule themselves. In the end, Smuts' proposal was not implemented in Europe, but only in territories of the Ottoman and German Empires outside Europe (Bentwich (n 169) 2). On Wilson's adoption of Smuts' proposal see Wright (n 169) 30-34; George Curry, 'Woodrow Wilson, Jan Smuts, and the Versailles Settlement' (1961) 66 *American Historical Review* 968; Karin Loevy, 'Reinventing a Region (1915-22): Visions of the Middle East in Legal and Diplomatic Texts Leading to the Palestine Mandate' (2016) 49 *Israel Law Review* 309, 332.

175 Pedersen (n 169) 27. Also see Strawson (n 166). Referring to international law at the time the Mandate was approved Strawson writes: "International law was at that time in a critical stage of its evolution but it remained a system of institutions and doctrines imprinted with its colonial origin" (ibid 53).

5.3 Article 22 of the League of Nations Covenant

Article 22 of the League of Nations Covenant that provided the legal basis for establishing a mandate states:

> To those colonies and territories which as a consequence of the late war have ceased to be under the sovereignty of the States which formerly governed them and which are inhabited by peoples not yet able to stand by themselves under the strenuous conditions of the modern world, there should be applied the principle that the well-being and development of such peoples form a sacred trust of civilization and that securities for the performance of this trust should be embodied in this Covenant.
> The best method of giving practical effect to this principle is that the tutelage of such peoples should be entrusted to advanced nations who by reason of their resources, their experience or their geographical position can best undertake this responsibility, and who are willing to accept it, and that this tutelage should be exercised by them as Mandatories on behalf of the League.
> The character of the mandate must differ according to the stage of the development of the people, the geographical situation of the territory, its economic conditions and other similar circumstances.
> Certain communities formerly belonging to the Turkish Empire have reached a stage of development where their existence as independent nations can be provisionally recognized subject to the rendering of administrative advice and assistance by a Mandatory until such time as they are able to stand alone. The wishes of these communities must be a principal consideration in the selection of the Mandatory.

In reading Article 22, a number of points must be stressed:

1. In governing territories inhabited by peoples who could not [in the minds of the colonial powers] govern themselves, the well-being and development of those peoples "form a sacred trust of civilization". No distinction is made between different groups of inhabitants of these territories. The sacred trust exists towards all peoples in the territories. This principle gains expression in the text of the British Mandate over Palestine. Article 2 declares that alongside its obligation to place the country under such conditions "as will secure the establishment of the national Jewish home", the Mandatory Power has the responsibility for "the development of self-governing institutions and also for safeguarding the civil and religious rights of all the inhabitants of Palestine, irrespec-

tive of race and religion." Article 15 states: "No discrimination of any kind shall be made between the inhabitants of Palestine on the ground of race, religion or language."

2. Certain communities that were formerly part of the Turkish Empire were provisionally recognized as independent nations, subject to temporary rule by the Mandatory powers. Mandates under this paragraph of article 22 became known as A mandates. Since until it was occupied by Britain, Palestine was part of the Turkish Empire, the Mandate of Britain over Palestine was an A mandate. The Mandate states expressly that it was entrusted to Great Britain "for the purpose of giving effect to the provisions of Article 22 of the Covenant of the League of Nations...".[176] In other words, the community in Palestine was provisionally recognized as an independent nation, and Britain was to govern the country according to "the principle that the well-being and development of [the people of Palestine] form a sacred trust of civilization."

While Palestine was provisionally recognized as a nation, the Mandate over Palestine also contained special provisions stating that Britain "should be responsible for putting into effect the declaration originally made on November 2nd, 1917, by the Government of His Britannic Majesty, and adopted by the said Powers, in favour of the establishment in Palestine of a national home for the Jewish people."[177] I now turn to the background and meaning of this commitment.

5.4 Balfour Declaration and San Remo Conference

In November 1917, the British Cabinet passed a resolution to adopt what later became known as the Balfour Declaration.[178] It is not my intention here to go into the background to this important document that has been

---

176 Preamble to The Palestine Mandate (1922) <https://avalon.law.yale.edu/20th_century/palmanda.asp> accessed 13 January 2025. The text of the League Covenant itself is available at <https://avalon.law.yale.edu/20th_century/leagcov.asp> accessed 13 January 2025.

177 ibid.

178 The Declaration appears in a letter sent by the Foreign Secretary, Arthur Balfour, to Lord Rothschild, a leader of the Jewish community in Great Britain: The Balfour Declaration (1917) <https://avalon.law.yale.edu/20th_century/balfour.asp> accesses 13 January 2025.

discussed by many others.[179] Suffice it to say that in the Balfour Declaration, Britain declared that it viewed "with favour the establishment in Palestine of a national home for the Jewish people, and will use their best endeavours to facilitate the achievement of this object, it being clearly understood that nothing shall be done which may prejudice the civil and religious rights of existing non-Jewish communities in Palestine, or the rights and political status enjoyed by Jews in any other country."[180]

Supporters of the idea that the Jews have an eternal right to settle in all parts of Palestine rest their view on the decision at the San Remo conference to include the Balfour Declaration in the Mandate over Palestine.[181] It is therefore important to clarify two points: one is that the San Remo conference was not a meeting of the League, but a meeting of the "Principal Allied Powers", namely the states that had been victorious in the war.[182] At this meeting it was decided that the Mandate over Palestine would be entrusted to Britain, and that it would include Britain's commitments

179 See, eg, Schneer (n 12); Karin Loevy, 'The Balfour Declaration's Territorial Landscape: Between Protection and Self-Determination' (2021) 12(2) *Humanity: An International Journal of Human Rights, Humanitarianism, and Development* 138; Shaul Arieli, "What did the Balfour Declaration Really Give to the Jewish People" *Ha'aretz* (31 October 2024) <https://www.haaretz.co.il/opinions/2024-10-31/ty-article-opinion/.premium/00000192-e247-dd31-a9be-fb4f69990000> accessed 13 January 2025.

180 The Balfour Declaration (n 178).

181 See, eg, Howard Grief, *The Legal Foundation and Borders of Israel under International Law* (Mazo Publishers 2008). As Professor Nathan Feinberg pointed out, had the Balfour Declaration stood on its own, it would have had no legal significance. Its legal significance rests on its inclusion in the Mandate: Nathan Feinberg, *On an Arab Jurist's Approach to Zionism and the State of Israel* (Magnes Press 1971) 22.

182 Together with the U.S., two representatives of each of these countries (Britain, France, Italy and Japan) had formed the Committee of Ten or Supreme Council that in effect ran the Paris Peace Conference: Margaret Macmillan (n 170) 53-57. In December 1919 the U.S. left the Committee of Ten and was invited to San Remo as an observer (Wright (n 169) 45, 54). On the background to the San Remo Conference see ibid 36-47. On the negotiations between Britain, France and Italy that led to the San Remo conference see A.E. Montgomery, 'The Making of the Treaty of Sevres of 10 August 1920' (1972) 15 *The Historical Journal* 775. The meetings between Britain, France, Italy and Japan were not held under the auspices of the League of Nations, and the San Remo conference was not a League of Nations conference. Also see Ephraim Karsh, *The San Remo Conference 100 years on; How the Jewish National Home Entered International Law* (Begin-Sadat Center for Strategic Studies 2020) <https://besacenter.org/wp-content/uploads/2020/04/172-MONOGRAPH-San-Remo-Conference-Karsh-FINAL.pdf> accessed 27 January 2025.

under the Balfour Declaration.[183] The Mandate itself states expressly that it was the Principal Allied Powers that decided to entrust the Mandate to Britain.[184]

The arrangements agreed by the Principal Allied Powers at San Remo were not incorporated in a written agreement and therefore they may not have had any legal, as opposed to political, force. Besides, even if a written agreement had been signed, it would only have bound the states that were parties to it, and not the whole international community.

5.5 Terms of the Mandate

Following San Remo, intense discussions took place between the British government and the Zionist leaders on the terms of the Mandate.[185] Despite the wishes of the Zionist leadership,[186] the Mandate does not refer to Palestine as the home of the Jewish people, but to the establishment of a national home for them **in** Palestine. Lord Curzon, who replaced Balfour as Foreign Secretary in 1919, was no fan of the Balfour Declaration and of Britain's assumption of the Mandate. He was adamant that the Mandate would not recognize that the Jews had a right or title to Palestine. Hence the Mandate does not refer to a right but includes Balfour's proposal that recognition be given "to the historical connection of the Jewish people with Palestine and to the grounds for reconstituting their national home in that country."[187]

---

183 MacMillan (n 170) 406-407, writes: "At the San Remo conference in April 1920, where the terms of the treaty with the Ottoman empire were approved, the British and the French, their differences temporarily forgotten, awarded themselves mandates, the British for Palestine and Mesopotamia, the French for Syria. In theory these were not valid until they were confirmed by the League of Nations. Not surprisingly, a League dominated by Britain and France did this in 1922."

184 See Preamble to the Mandate (n 176).

185 John J McTague Jr, 'Zionist-British Negotiations over the Draft Mandate for Palestine, 1920' (1980) 42 *Jewish Social Studies* 281; Malcolm Yapp, 'The Making of the Palestine Mandate' (1995) 1 *Middle East Lectures* 9.

186 For discussion regarding suggestions made by the Zionist leaders, see McTague (n 185).

187 Yapp (n 185) argues that Lord Curzon would have liked to weaken the connection of the Jewish people even more, but was forced to accept Balfour's proposal that was incorporated in the Preamble to the Mandate. On Curzon's attitude see also Kattan (n 15) 122-125; David Gilmour, 'The Unregarded Prophet: Lord Curzon and the Palestine Question' (1996) 25 *Journal of Palestine Studies* 60.

In all events, the League had no authority to recognize the rights of peoples over territory. Furthermore, at the time the Mandate was approved international law did not recognize a **right** to self-determination. The fact that the Mandate did not recognize, neither explicitly nor implicitly, the legal right of the Jewish people to establish a state in Palestine[188] was made perfectly clear by Winston Churchill in the White Paper that he published shortly before the approval of the Mandate by the League's Council.[189]

Those who wish to challenge the right of the Palestinian people to self-determination, rely, inter alia, on the fact that there is no reference in the Mandate to the political rights of the non-Jewish communities, but only to their religious and civil rights.[190] This bothered the representatives of France and Italy during the discussions at San Remo and they agreed to include the Balfour Declaration in the Mandate only after Britain clarified that in its view the term "civil rights" (of the existing non-Jewish communities) includes political rights.[191] Furthermore, even if there is no express reference in the Mandate to the political rights of the non-Jewish communities, one cannot conclude that no such rights exist today, when the right to self-determination of peoples has gained the status of a peremptory norm of international law.

188 On the meaning of the national home for the Jewish people, see Karin Loevy (n 174). Loevy argues that what lay behind the Balfour Declaration was not the idea of a Jewish state in Palestine but "a European protected space in colonial territory". And see Pedersen (n 169) 359: "Neither the Balfour Declaration nor the Mandate for Palestine promised a Jewish state. Nor did those founding texts promise a Jewish 'national home'. What they promised, rather, was that the British government would 'look with favour'... on the Jewish effort to create that home themselves."

189 *British White Paper* (n 21).

190 Rostow, 'Correspondence' (n 154) 718: 'The term "civil rights" in that sentence is carefully distinguished from political rights'; Einhorn (n 156).

191 Pedersen (n 169) 35. In assuming that the term 'civil rights' was carefully distinguished from political rights, Rostow seemed oblivious both to the fact that this term was taken from the Balfour Declaration, and that when the issue was raised the British made clear that in their view the term 'civil rights' includes 'political rights.' In 1922 there was no recognised right of peoples to self-determination, nor recognition of international human rights. The term 'political rights' therefore obviously referred to rights within the domestic legal system, first and foremost amongst which was the right to vote and to stand for election. In arguing that the Mandate did not recognise the 'political rights' of non-Jewish communities in Palestine, it seems unlikely that Rostow was arguing that were there to be elections in Palestine, only Jews would be able to vote and to stand for election. Such an interpretation would have stood in stark contrast to Article 15 of the Mandate that states: "No discrimination of any kind shall be made between the inhabitants of Palestine on the ground of race, religion or language."

Britain undertook to facilitate establishment of a home for the Jewish people in Palestine although they were well aware that they were violating Wilson's principle of self-determination.[192] This does not mean, however, that one may interpret the Mandate as an instrument that deals with the interests of the Jews, and their interests alone. Under Article 22 the well-being of the *peoples* in a Mandate territory was a "sacred trust".[193] The claim that the Mandate was a special case which departed from this principle is incompatible both with Article 22 and with the express statement in the opening paragraph of the Mandate, that it was being entrusted to Great Britain "with the purpose of giving effect to Article 22". It also lends support to those who claim that the Mandate was unlawful since if it was not aimed to fulfill the "sacred trust" there was no legal basis for entrusting it to Britain.[194]

5.6 Approval of the Mandate by League's Council

While Foreign Minister Curzon was not in favour of Britain assuming the Mandate, Prime Minister Lloyd George supported the idea. Hence the task of getting League approval for the Mandate was entrusted to Balfour.[195] Balfour faced resistance from some members of the League.[196] Article 5 of the League's Covenant adopted the principle of unanimity for decisions of both the League Council and its Assembly. The Covenant did not provide which body was to approve a Mandate and Balfour feared that if the decision were in the hands of the Assembly, in which all League members had a vote, the Mandate might not be approved. He therefore demanded

192 See eg, the letter of Lord Balfour to Prime Minister Lloyd George of 19 February 1919 in which Balfour wrote: "The weak point of our position, of course, is that in the case of Palestine we deliberately and rightly decline to accept the principle of self-determination." (cited in Kattan (n 15) 121. Also see Kattan, ibid 122-125).

193 As Pedersen (n 169) 359 points out "the mandate instructed Britain to establish a common Palestinian citizenship and to foster self-governing institutions for the population as a whole".

194 Quigley (n 167).

195 Susan Pedersen, 'Writing the Balfour Declaration into the Mandate for Palestine' (2022) 45 *International History Review* 279. After being replaced as Foreign Secretary by Lord Curzon, Balfour remained in the Cabinet as Lord President of the Council.

196 For example, the Vatican, which opposed the Mandate since it feared Jewish and Muslim control over the Christian holy places, had a strong influence over Italy and, it would seem, over other Catholic members of the League too: Pedersen, ibid 286.

that the decision should be in the hands of the Council, in which there were only eight members, including all four of the Principal Allied Powers that had approved the Mandate at San Remo.[197] He managed to obtain France's agreement to this move, on condition that the Mandate over Palestine would not enter into force until France's Mandate over Syria and Lebanon was approved.[198] After discussion of the draft which Britain submitted, in the course of which the members of the Council reached agreement on the wording, on 24 July 1922 the Council approved the Mandate, but delayed its entry into force until France and Italy reached agreement on the French Mandate.[199] After these two countries informed the Council that they had reached an agreement, the Council decided on 29 September 1923 that both the British Mandate over Palestine and the French Mandate over Syria would enter into force immediately.[200]

The fact that the Mandate was confirmed by the Council, rather than the Assembly of the League of Nations, is significant. In his letter dated 19 June 2023 the Cabinet Secretary, displaying unfortunate ignorance, states that the Mandate was approved unanimously by the League of Nations at San Remo.[201] As stated above, the San Remo conference was not a conference of the League, and the Mandate was not approved by the League at San Remo. But perhaps more important is the fact that the Mandate was approved by the Council, which was comprised of only 8 of the 51 members of the League.[202] Thus, one cannot even argue that approval of the declaration on "the historical connection of the Jewish people with Palestine and to the rounds for reconstituting their national home in that country" is evidence of support for this declaration by the majority of states that were members of the League, let alone that it achieved unanimous support of the League of Nations.

197 ibid.

198 ibid.

199 *League of Nations, Official Journal, Minutes of Thirteenth (Public) Meeting of Council, held at St. James Palace, London, on Monday July 24th 1922 at 3 pm.*

200 *League of Nations, Official Journal, Minutes of Twenty-Third Meeting of Council, held at Geneva on Saturday September 29th 1923 at 10:30 am.*

201 See letter 19.6.2023 (n 140).

202 Besides the Principal Allied Powers (Britain, France, Italy and Japan) the other members were Belgium, Brazil, China and Spain.

5.7 Legal Status of the Mandate

A League of Nations mandate was an international agreement between the League and the Mandatory power.[203] There is nothing in the League of Nations Covenant to suggest that decisions of the League Council, such as the approval of a Mandate, bound all members of the League, not to mention states who were not members when the decision was made. At the time, the legal doctrine in international law was that an international agreement does not give rights, or impose duties, on persons or states who were not parties to the agreement.[204] This view was reflected many years later in a judgment of the Supreme Court of Israel.[205]

Under Article 26 of the British Mandate over Palestine, Britain agreed that if any dispute were to arise between it and a member of the League of Nations regarding implementation or interpretation of the Mandate, if the dispute could not be settled by negotiation, the Permanent Court of International Justice would have jurisdiction to deal with it. One could argue that the implication was that the commitments of the Mandatory Power were not only to the League, but to all its members. This argument was rejected by the ICJ in the South West Africa case. The Court held that the provision in Article 26, which also appeared in the mandate of South Africa over Namibia, did not mean that the mandatory power had a

---

203 *South West Africa Cases (Ethiopia v South Africa; Liberia v South Africa)* (Preliminary Objections) [1962] ICJ Rep. 319, 331 ("The Mandate, in fact and in law, is an international agreement having the character of a treaty or convention. It is an instrument having the character of a treaty or convention and embodying international engagements for the Mandatory as defined by the Council and accepted by the Mandatory.").

204 Wright (n 169) 119) explains that since the populations of the mandatory area were not parties to the agreement, they were not able to acquire rights according to it. And see art 34 of the Vienna Convention on the Law of Treaties (23 May 1969) 1155 UNTS 331, that relates to the obligations and rights of party states. On developments in international law regarding the rights of the individual see Anne Peters, *Beyond Human Rights: The Legal Status of the Individual in International Law* (CUP 2016) ch 2.

205 C.A. 22/55 *Custodian of Absentee Property v Samara* [12 December 1956]. In this case the respondent was the resident of a village in the "Triangle" that was included on the Israeli side of the Armistice Line with Jordan. In challenging the order expropriating his property the respondent relied on Israel's commitment in the Armistice Agreement to respect the property rights of villagers in the "Triangle". The Supreme Court held that a third party had no rights under the Agreement that only bound the states that were parties to it.
s.

general legal obligation towards each member state of the League to fulfil its obligations under the mandate.[206]

5.8 Right of Jews to Settle in the Land of Israel

The main legal argument of those who have advanced the right of Jews to settle in the West Bank after Israel gained control over the area in 1967 rests on the British Mandate. This argument rests on three propositions:

a. The Mandate recognized a **right** of Jews to settle in all parts of Mandatory Palestine;
b. That right was a right *erga omnes*;
c. That right continues to exist after the British Mandate ended.

As we have seen above, the British refused to include in the Mandate reference to the right or title of Jews, or of the Jewish people, to establish a home in Palestine. Britain undertook to encourage settlement of Jews on the land in Palestine, subject to the obligation to ensure that other sections of the population were not prejudiced.[207] Even assuming that the Mandate did grant a right to Jews, who were the intended beneficiaries of the Mandate, their right regarding settlement was the right to demand that Britain encourage such settlement; it was not a right to settle in all parts of Palestine. This right towards Britain could not be, and was not, a right *erga omnes*. It was a right that ended when the Mandate itself ended.

5.9 Article 80 of the UN Charter and the Trusteeship Argument

The Charter of the United Nations, which replaced the dissolved League of Nations, does not retain the Mandate system. Instead it recognizes the possibility of subjecting certain territories, including those held under a mandate, to a trusteeship.[208] Article 80 addresses the question of the status

206 *South West Africa Cases (Ethiopia v South Africa; Liberia v South Africa)* (Second Phase, Judgment) [1966] ICJ. Rep 6. It must be admitted that this judgment was highly controversial. The Court was evenly split and the decision was based on a casting vote of the Court's president.

207 See Pedersen (n 169) 359.

208 Art 77 of the UN Charter.

of mandate territories that had not been made subject to a trusteeship.[209] According to this article, even though the League of Nations, which had approved the Mandate, no longer existed, Britain was still obligated to comply with its undertakings under the Mandate. To the extent Jews had a right to demand that Britain fulfil its Mandate obligations, *this* right continued to exist after the League of Nations was dissolved and no trusteeship had been established in place of the Mandate. When the Mandate ended with the approval of the UN General Assembly, Britain no longer had any obligations under the Mandate and so obviously, the right to demand that it fulfil its Mandate obligations was no longer relevant.

Professor Rostow argued that the Mandate continued after the Mandatory Power no longer had control over Palestine, and that it would be terminated only if the territory were made subject to a UN trusteeship or if another state were established in the area. He based the argument on the Advisory Opinion in the *Namibia* case.[210] In that case, South Africa continued its control over Namibia even though its mandate over the territory had been terminated by the General Assembly. In this context, the ICJ held that South Africa was bound by the duties of a trustee over the territory. One cannot conclude that territory that was ruled under a League of Nations mandate is subject to some form of trust even when, with the consent of the General Assembly, the mandatory power has ended the mandate and no longer maintains control over the territory.

Rostow's argument ignores the fact that the mandate system was created in order to give a particular state the "mandate" to administer a territory until it became independent. It was not a system to define the status of territories that were no longer part of a recognized state, but a mechanism for provisional administration over a territory that had been part of a defeated empire until the principle of self-determination could be implemented.[211] When the UN General Assembly confirmed Britain's decision to terminate the Mandate, it recommended that the people of Palestine should exercise their right to self-determination in two states: a Jewish state and an Arab

209 See Shaw (n 169) 303.

210 Rostow (n 142).

211 See the definition of "Mandate" in the MPEPIL: "The mandate system was created in the aftermath of World War I to resolve the question of jurisdiction over the colonial territories detached from the defeated nations of Germany and the Ottoman (Turkish) Empire...Under this system, selected nation States were granted mandates to govern selected territories on behalf of the League of Nations." (Ruth Gordon, 'Mandates' in *Max Planck Encyclopedias of International Law* (2013)).

state. The United Nations could have decided to subject the territory of Palestine to a Trusteeship, but although the US submitted a plan for it to do so,[212] the proposal was dropped after Israel declared its independence.[213] The fact that a Palestinian state was not established in 1948 in no way diminishes from the right of the Palestinians in the part of Palestine that did not become part of Israel to exercise their right to self-determination.

5.10 General Assembly Resolution 181

The UN General Assembly did not have the authority to make a binding decision regarding the future government of Palestine after the Mandate ended. Hence, the widely held view is that the Partition Plan was a recommendation.[214] This does not mean that the General Assembly did not have the authority to approve Britain's decision to end the Mandate.

In the *Namibia* Advisory Opinion, the ICJ held that the General Assembly had the authority to terminate South Africa's mandate over Namibia due to South Africa's violation of its terms.[215] It follows that the General Assembly must also have had the authority to approve the decision of the mandatory power to end the mandate. It is therefore the considered opinion of virtually all experts that the Mandate over Palestine ended on the day Britain withdrew its forces from the country, namely 15 May 1948, which is the day Israel became an independent state.[216] This view was expressed in a judgment of the Supreme Court of Israel.[217] The ICJ also

---

212 Thomas J Hamilton, 'U.S. Trustee Plan for Palestine Gets Cool U.N. Greeting' *New York Times* (21 April 1948) <https://www.nytimes.com/1948/04/21/archives/us-trustee-plan-for-palestine-gets-cool-un-greeting-new-zealand.html> accessed 15 January 2025.

213 Gail J Boling, 'The U.S.- Proposed "Trustee Agreement" for Palestine: The UN-Styled Plan That Could Have Avoided Forcible Displacement of the Palestinian Refugees in 1948' (2003) 21(2) *Refuge* 70.

214 Some scholars were indeed of the opinion that the resolution was binding, but the common view is that it was merely a recommendation. See Robbie Sabel, *International Law and the Arab-Israeli Conflict* (CUP 2022) 93; Feinberg (n 181).

215 *Namibia* Advisory Opinion (n 143).

216 Sabel (n 214); Feinberg (n 181) 121; Shaw (n 169) 303; Crawford (n 49) 567, 580.

217 HCJ 222/68 *Chugim Leumi'im v Minister of Police* [1970] (PD 24(2) 141, para 18 in judgment of Justice Silberg ("The "establishment of the State" and "the end of the Mandate" are one and the same thing. Since the State was established when the Mandate ended, and the Mandate ended when the State was established").

opined that the Mandate ended when Britain withdrew from Palestine.[218] From its decisions on issues connected with the post-1967 situation in the West Bank it is clear that this is the view of the UN Security Council too.[219] Israel never raised the claim that the Mandate continues to apply in parts of Eretz-Yisrael/Palestine which are not part of its sovereign territory. It accepted UNSC Resolution 242 of November 1967 in which there is not a hint that some of the territories Israel occupied in 1967 are still subject to the terms of a League Mandate. The subsequent Security Council resolutions on the illegality of the Israeli settlements in the West Bank are also not consistent with the idea that the Mandate still applies in the area.

5.11 The Mandate and other International Instruments

One of the inexplicable assumptions implicit in the Rostow argument is that the Mandate is some kind of "supra international document" that trumps all subsequent developments in international law, including decisions of the most important international organs, foremost amongst which is the UN Security Council.

I write that this is an assumption, since none of the people who have supported the "Mandate argument" have ever explained on what theory they base the primacy of the Mandate.[220] Unlike Article 25 of the UN Charter that provides that decisions of the Security Council bind all member states, there was no provision in the League of Nations Covenant under which decisions of the Council or Assembly bound members. Furthermore, unlike Article 103 of the UN Charter that gives priority to a UN member's Charter obligations over the member's other treaty obligations, the League Covenant did not give primacy to members' Covenant obligations.

There are numerous resolutions of the UN General Assembly and Security Council declaring that Israel is an occupying power in the West Bank

---

218 *Wall* Advisory Opinion (n 82) para 162.

219 See UNSC Resolutions listed above in n 8.

220 Professor Nathan Feinberg wrote in 1936 that by its approval of the Mandate, the League of Nations obliged the member states to help Britain fulfill its Mandate obligations, and in any case, they had to refrain from doing anything to prevent Britain from fulfilling its role. Feinberg did not provide any reference for this opinion, and eventually narrowed down this opinion (Nathan Feinberg, *Some Problems of the Palestine Mandate* (Shoshani's Printing 1936) 113). Since Britain's obligations lost their validity with the end of the Mandate, it is clear that the obligations of other countries (according to Feinberg's view) had no meaning either.

and that as such it is bound by its obligations under the Fourth Geneva Convention. Leaving aside the General Assembly resolutions, which are not legally binding, a strong case can be made out that at least some of the Security Council resolutions include decisions that are binding. Article 25 of the Charter stipulates that the member states accept and agree to carry out all "decisions" of the Security Council. In the *Namibia* case, the ICJ rejected South Africa's argument that only Security Council resolutions passed under Chapter VII of the Charter are binding.[221] Even resolutions passed under Chapter VI may be binding, all depending on the Council's intention, as reflected, inter alia, in the language used in the resolution.[222] Hence, for example, in UNSC Resolution 2334 (23 December 2016) the Security Council reiterated its "**demand** that Israel immediately and completely cease all settlement activities in the occupied Palestinian territory, including East Jerusalem, and that it fully respect all of its legal obligations in this regard." (emphasis added). Use of the term "demand", as opposed to the term "calls upon", used in other parts of the same resolution, may very well imply that the SC intended that this be a binding decision.[223]

---

221 *Namibia* Advisory Opinion (n 143).

222 Rosalyn Higgins, 'The Advisory Opinion on Namibia: Which UN Resolutions are Binding under Article 25 of the Charter?' (1972) 21(2) *International & Comparative Law Quarterly* 270-286, who argues that there is no basis in the text of the Charter to suggest that only decisions adopted under the Security Council's powers under Chapter VII of the Charter are binding. Also see para 51 in the joint opinion of Judges Tomka, Abraham and Aurescu in Advisory Opinion: *Occupied Palestinian Territory* (n 9): "It is important to note that not only the resolutions adopted under Chapter VII of the Charter of the United Nations are binding. As the Court has explained in the *Namibia* Advisory Opinion, a careful analysis of the language of a resolution is required before a conclusion can be made as to its binding effect...".

223 Joint opinion of Judges Tomka, Abraham and Aurescu, ibid; Dan Joyner, 'Legal Bindingness of Security Council Resolutions Generally, and Resolution 2334 on the Israeli Settlements in Particular' *EJIL:Talk*! (9 January 2017) <https://tinyurl.com/2528nuvk> accessed 15 January 2025; Abraham Joseph, 'Why the UN Resolution on Israeli Settlements is Binding' *The Wire* (30 December 2016) <https://thewire.in/world/un-resolution-israeli-settlements-binding> accessed 15 January 2025. cf Orde F. Kittrie, 'What UNSCR 2334 Could Mean Beyond the United Nations, and How the Trump Administration Can Respond' *LAWFARE* (27 December 2016) <https://www.lawfaremedia.org/article/what-unscr-2334-could-mean-beyond-united-nations-and-how-trump-administration-can-respond> accessed 15 January 2025. The debate on whether specific SC resolutions relating to the Israel/Palestine conflict are binding has continued: see Eiran Sthoeger, 'Resolution 2728 on Israel/Gaza is Significant, But it is Not a Binding Council Decision' *EJIL:Talk*! (26 April 2024) <https://www.ejiltalk.org/resolution-2728-on-israel-gaza-is-significant-but-it-is-not-a-binding-council-decision/> accessed 15 January 2025; Eirik Bjorge, 'Resolution 2728 (2024)

International law did not freeze in 1922, when the British Mandate over Palestine was approved by the Council of the League of Nations. Much has happened in international law since 1922. In the present context, the most important developments are the total rejection of colonialism and colonial regimes and the development of the right of peoples to self-determination. Resting Israel's rights in the West Bank and its right to settle its citizens there on what was, as we saw above, essentially a colonial regime, and denying the right to self-determination of the other people who live in the land, might have been persuasive arguments 100 years ago. In the world of the 21st Century, their only effect is to lend credence to the growing number of people in the world who claim that Israel is a colonial regime.

The question of the continued validity of an international instrument that is no longer compatible with customary international law arose in the *Namibia case*, concerning South Africa's mandate over Namibia. In that case the ICJ held that "an international instrument has to be interpreted and applied within the framework of the entire legal system prevailing at the time of the interpretation." [224]

The potential tension between instruments that were valid under the prevailing norms of international law at the time they were made, and subsequent developments in international law, was mentioned by Max Huber in his famous decision in the Palmas Islands Arbitration.[225] In this decision Huber mentioned two parts to the intertemporal principle: the creation of rights and the continued existence of rights. While the creation of a right is determined by the law in force at the time it was created, "the existence of the right, in other words its continued manifestation, shall follow the conditions required by the evolution of law."[226] In our context, even if we were to assume that the Mandate created the right of Jews to settle in

is a Binding Council Resolution' *EJIL:Talk!* (26 April 2024) <https://www.ejiltalk.org/resolution-2728-2024-is-a-binding-council-resolution/> accessed 15 January 2025; Akira Kato, 'Really Binding? Security Council Resolution 2728 (2024) and Non-State Actors' *EJIL:Talk!* (9 September 2024) <https://www.ejiltalk.org/really-binding-security-council-resolution-2728-2024-and-non-state-actors/> accessed 15 January 2025.

224 *Namibia* Advisory Opinion (n 143) para 53.

225 *Islands of Palmas case (Netherlands v US)* (4 April 1928) II *Reports of International Arbitral Awards* 829.

226 ibid 845. On this distinction of Huber, see Steven Wheatley, 'Revisiting the Doctrine of Intertemporal Law' (2021) 41 *Oxford Journal of Legal Studies* 484. On relevance of the intertemporal principle in the context of the Israel-Palestine conflict see Strawson (n 166).

all parts of Palestine (an assumption, it will be recalled, that I rejected above), the continued existence of that right must take into account subsequent developments in international law.[227] These developments include the prohibition on acquisition of territory by use of force, the right to self-determination of peoples and the prohibition on an occupying power to transfer part of its civilian population into occupied territory.

5.12 Concluding Comments on Mandate Argument

In ending my criticism of Rostow's "Mandate argument", three points are worth mentioning. Rostow presented his view before the competent organs of the UN expressed their opinion on the matter. Rostow assigned major significance to the Advisory Opinion of the ICJ in the *Namibia* case and even criticised those who attacked this Opinion as being based on colonial ideas.[228] Rostow passed away before the ICJ delivered two Advisory Opinions in which it held that the West Bank (including East Jerusalem) is subject to a regime of belligerent occupation.[229] Is it fair to assume that Rostow would have given these Opinions the same weight he gave to the *Namibia* Opinion, even if he disagreed with the Court's reasoning?

Secondly, in deciding on the position of international law on a given question, the greatest weight must be given to decisions of international organs, first and foremost amongst which are the International Court of Justice and the UN Security Council, and to that of states. In issues of international law before the International Court of Justice, the views of academic experts may serve only as "subsidiary means for the determination of the

227 As the ICJ stated in the *Namibia* Advisory Opinion (n 143) para 53: "Mindful as it is of the primary necessity of interpreting an instrument in accordance with the intentions of the parties at the time of its conclusion, the Court is bound to take into account the fact that the concepts embodied in Article 22 of the Covenant-"the strenuous conditions of the modern world" and "the well-being and development" of the peoples concerned-were not static, but were by definition evolutionary, as also, therefore, was the concept of the "sacred trust". The parties to the Covenant must consequently be deemed to have accepted them as such."

228 Rostow (n 142).

229 See Advisory Opinion, *Occupied Palestinian Territory* (n 9) *Wall* Advisory Opinion (n 82).

rules of international law",[230] but they cannot prevail when contrary to the position of the Court itself, the UN Security Council, and most states.

Finally, let us assume for the moment that the "sacred trust" created by the Mandate over Palestine continues in force after the Mandate ended. What are the implications? As mentioned above, the "sacred trust" mentioned in Article 22 of the League Covenant was a sacred trust to all the peoples in the mandated territories until such time as they would gain their independence. The Jews in Eretz Yisrael/Palestine have gained their independence. The other people in the territory – the Palestinian Arabs – have not. Hence the implications of Rostow's view is that the UN has a duty to make sure that the trust is not abused and that the Palestinians who are subjects of the sacred trust will obtain their independence too. This was indeed the view taken by the International Court of Justice in its Advisory Opinion in the Wall case. The ICJ stated:

> The responsibility of the United Nations in this matter also has its origin in the Mandate and the Partition Resolution concerning Palestine... This responsibility has been described by the General Assembly as "a permanent responsibility towards the question of Palestine until the question is resolved in all its aspects in a satisfactory manner in accordance with international legitimacy" (General Assembly resolution 571107 of 3 December 2002). Within the institutional framework of the Organization, this responsibility has been manifested by the adoption of many Security Council and General Assembly resolutions, and by the creation of several subsidiary bodies specifically established to assist in the realization of the inalienable rights of the Palestinian people.[231]

I doubt whether the Government of Israel, which so eagerly embraces Rostow's argument on the continued application of the Mandate trust in the

230 Art 38 of the Statute of the International Court of Justice that specifies the sources to which the ICJ must resort in deciding disputes on the basis of international law.

231 *Wall* Advisory Opinion (n 82) para 49. See also Committee on the Exercise of the Inalienable Rights of the Palestinian People, *Study: The Legality of the Israeli Occupation of the Occupied Palestinian Territory, Including East Jerusalem* (20 September 2023) UN Doc A/78/378, p. 29. In its report this UN committee accepts Rostow's argument that the trust over Palestine continues after the end of the Mandate. The Committee claims, however, that Rostow ignored Article 5 of the Mandate that states that the Mandatory Power must ensure that no part of the area is transferred to the sovereignty of a foreign government. The Committee argues that in the area that is not part of its territory, Israel is a foreign power that may not transfer part of its population into the area of the trust.

parts of Palestine that did not become part of Israel or Jordan, subscribes to this view.

Chapter 6: Judicial Review by Israel Supreme Court

6.1 Jurisdiction and Applicable Law

Soon after the 1967 War, Palestinian residents of the newly occupied territories petitioned the Israel Supreme Court, sitting as a High Court of Justice that exercises review over administrative action, in attempts to challenge the legality of measures adopted by the military authorities in those territories. The authorities did not challenge the Court's jurisdiction to consider such petitions, and the Court later ruled that its jurisdiction is based on its statutory power to issue orders against "all persons exercising public functions under law."[232] In the years that have passed the Court has considered thousands of petitions by Palestinian residents of the West Bank and other territories occupied in 1967. The Court's role in considering these petitions is arguably the most important development in the legal approach of the authorities to their actions in the territories occupied in 1967.[233]

Having conceded the Court's jurisdiction to consider petitions by Palestinians, the authorities were forced to decide on their approach to legal arguments raised by the petitioners that relied on the international law of belligerent occupation, as reflected both in the Hague Regulations and GCIV. Their initial approach was what may be termed a "pragmatic approach", the object of which was to avoid a judicial ruling on the application of the international law of belligerent occupation in the West Bank. Counsel for the authorities informed the Court that while the authorities did not concede that the military authorities were indeed bound by the provisions of the Hague Regulations and GCIV, they were convinced that their actions were compatible with these provisions, and they therefore agreed that the Court review their actions accordingly.[234] Most of the judges were willing to "play this game". One judge, Justice Alfred Witkon, was not. He explained that the High Court of Justice is not an arbitrator who may decide a case

232 Section 7(b)(2) of *Courts Law*, 1967, now Section 15(b)(2) of *Basic Law: The Judiciary* (1984).

233 For a full and comprehensive and critical discussion on the way the Court has exercised this jurisdiction see Kretzmer and Ronen (n 57).

234 HCJ 337/71 *Christian Society for the Holy Places v Minister of Defence* [1972] PD 26(1) 574; HCJ 302/72 *Abu Helou v Government of Israel* [1973] PD 27(2) 169.

on the basis of the parties' consent; it is a court of law that must rule according to the law that binds the parties.[235] The government had not given an undertaking to accept this legal framework in all cases, and Justice Witkon obviously feared that the government would adopt the "pragmatic approach" when it thought it had a strong case, but would refuse its consent when its case under the regime of belligerent occupation was weak.

Justice Witkon had no doubt that the rules that bind the authorities are the rules of the international law of belligerent occupation.[236] Nevertheless, he had a problem in enforcing these rules in a national court. His problem arose from the existing jurisprudence of the Court regarding the place of international law in Israel's domestic legal system.[237]

Soon after the State of Israel was established the Supreme Court adopted the traditional English approach to the relationship between domestic law and international law. According to this approach, customary international law is part of the common law of the land that will be enforced by the courts, unless it is clearly incompatible with parliamentary legislation. However, as the power to ratify international treaties on behalf of the state is in the hands of the executive branch of government, treaties that bind the state will not be enforced unless they, or the norms contained therein, have been incorporated in domestic law by parliamentary legislation.[238]

Without examining how relevant this distinction between customary and treaty law is when it comes to occupied territory, in which all power, including legislative power, is in the hands of the executive, the Court held that it would not enforce the norms of treaty law.[239] The initial assumption was that the norms of both the Hague Regulations and GCIV are not part

235 HCJ 302/72, ibid 181.

236 See HCJ 606/78 *Ayoub v Minister of Defence* [1979] PD 33(2) 113, 117 (hereinafter: *Beth El* case), in which Justice Witkon declared: "We are dealing with the rights of the parties before us according to the situation that prevails between Israel and the Arab states. That situation is one of belligerency and the status of the respondents [the minister of defence and two military commanders DK] towards the occupied territory is that of an occupying power."

237 *Abu Helou* case (n 234) 180.

238 David Kretzmer, 'International Law in Domestic Courts: Israel' in David Sloss (ed), *The Role of Domestic Courts in Treaty Enforcement: A Comparative Study* (CUP 2009) 273.

239 See *Abu Helou* case (n 234); *Beth El* case (n 236). In *Al-'Afou* case (n 109) the Court rejected the claim of the petitioners' counsel that the distinction between domestic enforcement of customary law and treaty law is not relevant in regard to the state's actions in occupied territory. The argument was that this distinction relies on a constitutional principle regarding separation of powers that is irrelevant in

of customary international law and so they will not be enforced by the Court.[240] After Professor Yoram Dinstein pointed out that the Nuremburg Tribunal had decided that the Hague Regulations had become part of customary international law,[241] the Court admitted that it had been mistaken and ruled that the Hague Regulations are indeed part of customary law, which may be enforced by the Court.[242] This became the accepted jurisprudence of the Court – since they reflect customary international law, the Court will enforce the Hague Regulations.[243]

The Court's pragmatic approach could not last long. Things came to a head in the famous *Elon Moreh* case.[244] In this case the government of PM Menachem Begin, which was committed to settlement of Jews in the whole of the historical land of Israel, gave in to demands of the *Gush Emunim* settler movement to establish a settlement in Samaria.[245] The Cabinet Committee on Settlement decided that the settlement would be established on private land of Palestinians, and the military commander of the area issued an order seizing the land for military purposes. The Palestinian land-owners challenged the seizure order in court, arguing, inter alia, that the order was incompatible with the military commander's powers under customary international law. As the settlers were likely to be affected by the Court's decision, the Court granted them permission to join the proceedings. Their counsel argued that the international law of belligerent occupation was irrelevant for two reasons: a) the land of Israel belongs to the people of Israel and cannot be regarded as occupied territory; and b) since Jordan was not the rightful sovereign of the territory in 1967, the territory did not become occupied territory when the IDF gained control over it in a war of self-defence.[246]

---

occupied territory in which all powers are in the hands of the executive branch of government.

240 *Abu Helou* case (n 234).

241 Yoram Dinstein, 'The Judgment in the *Rafah Approach* Case' (1974) 3 *Iyunei Mishpat* 934 [in Hebrew].

242 *Beth El* case (n 236). As Israel never joined the 1907 Hague Convention, it is not clear why the Hague Regulations should have applied to Israel's actions, unless they had become part of customary international law.

243 Kretzmer and Ronen (n 57) 63-64.

244 *Elon Moreh* case (n 151).

245 On the *Gush Emunim* movement and its influence on the settlement policy of the government see Akiva Eldar and Idit Zertal, *Lords of the land : the war over Israel's settlements in the occupied territories, 1967-2007* (Nation Books 2007) 188-244.

246 It will be recalled that this argument was originally raise by Yehuda Blum, 'The Missing Reversioner' (n 104), although Blum restricted the argument to application

The Court's answer to this argument signals its departure from the "pragmatic approach". The Court stated that the only legal basis for the military commander's order seizing the property was the power under international law of a military commander in occupied territory to seize land for military purposes. Hence, if the Court were to accept the settlers' argument that international law was irrelevant, it would have to rule that the military commander's order was ultra vires.[247]

In the *Elon Moreh* case Justice Landau attempted to distinguish between Blum's argument that Jordan was not the sovereign power in the West Bank when it was occupied by Israel in 1967, and the issue of the legal regime that applies in the territory. He stated that:

> One should recall...the important argument which Israel has voiced in the international arena. The argument rests on the fact that upon entry of the IDF into Judea and Samaria, this area was not held by any sovereign whose hold on the territory had gained international recognition.[248]

Despite this "reservation" Justice Landau held that the case could only be decided in accordance with the presumptions behind the Requisition Order. Hence, he held that the validity of that Order must be judged "according to the international law from which the military commander who issued it derives his powers."[249] The relevant international law is customary international law as reflected in the section of the Hague Regulations relating to occupied territory.

A short while later, in the *Ha'etzni* case, an Israeli settler who was being charged with a number of criminal offences before a military court in the West Bank petitioned the Supreme Court. Relying on Blum's article[250] the settler's counsel argued that since Jordan was not sovereign in the West Bank when it was occupied by Israel in 1967, the Jordanian laws that had been applied in the West Bank between 1949 and 1967 were null and void. His client therefore could not be charged with crimes under the Jordanian

---

of those parts of the law of belligerent occupation that aim to preserve the rights of the missing state sovereign (as opposed to humanitarian rights of the local population).

247 See *Elon Moreh* case (n 151) paras 12, 28. In the end the Court held that the dominant reason for the order seizing the land was political, rather than military, and that therefore the order was incompatible both with international law and Israeli administrative law.

248 ibid para 13.

249 ibid.

250 See n 104.

criminal code that was applied in the area before Israel conquered it. Justice Landau dismissed the argument. Once again, he attempted to distinguish between the issue of the sovereignty over the territory, and the application of the laws of belligerent occupation. He explained that one must not confuse:

> the question of the sovereignty in Judea and Samaria under international law, and the right and duty of the military to maintain public order in the area, so as to ensure his control over the area and to institute a regime based on the rule of law for the benefit of the inhabitants there. This right and this duty, which are derived from customary international law, are expressed in article 43 of the Hague Regulations.[251]

In truth it is quite difficult to make sense of this. The fact that the rule in Article 43 is part of customary law does not explain why it applies to the situation in the West Bank. Article 43 only applies in territory that is occupied territory, as defined in Article 42 of the Hague Regulations. If a court relies on Article 43 it necessarily implies that the territory is occupied territory. In other words, while mentioning Blum's reservation about the applicable legal regime, the Court rejected Blum's conclusion that the whole of the law of belligerent occupation does not apply in the West Bank. In fact, it conceded application of the Hague Regulations that are based partly on protecting the rights of the legitimate sovereign, rather than the humanitarian rights of the population in the area. The Court added to this confusion when it added that the implications of Blum's analysis is the government argument that GCIV does not apply to Israel's actions in the West Bank.[252] But the implications of Blum's analysis should have been quite the opposite: that part of the Hague Regulations whose object is to protect the rights of the missing sovereign does not apply, whereas the Geneva Convention, which is a purely humanitarian convention, applies.

The *Elon Moreh* and *Ha'etzni* decisions exposed the inherent limitations of the "pragmatic approach". As long as the authorities relied on this approach merely to accept restrictions on their powers that did not necessarily bind them, the approach could be maintained. However, as soon as the argument concerned the very power of the military commander to take a person's private property (or to violate other rights, such as prosecuting a person for an act that does not constitute a crime under the prevailing law),

251 HCJ 61/80 *Ha'etzni v Minister of Defence* [1980]s PD34 (3) 595, 597.
252 ibid.

the "pragmatic approach" became untenable. The Court clearly realized this. Since the *Elon Moreh* case it has ruled time and again that the legal regime in the West Bank is a regime of belligerent occupation.[253]

Thus, for example, in the leading case of *Jami'yat Iskan* (1983), the Court stated:

> Judea and Samaria are held by Israel by way of military occupation or belligerent occupation. In the area, a military government was established at the head of which is the military commander. The powers and authority of the military commander are derived from the rules of public international law that deal with belligerent occupation...[254]

In a joint judgment delivered in 2005 by ten of the eleven judges on the bench, in referring to the West Bank and Gaza, the Court stated:

> According to the legal outlook of all Israel's governments as presented to this court—an outlook that has always been accepted by the Supreme Court—these areas are held by Israel by way of belligerent occupation. . . . The legal regime that applies there is determined by the rules of public international law and especially the rules relating to belligerent occupation.[255]

As we shall see below, there is clear dissonance between the law, as described by the Supreme Court, and practice. Ignoring that dissonance for the moment, it must be emphasized that ruling that the West Bank is subject to a regime of belligerent occupation did not mean that the Court was prepared in principle to enforce all the norms of that regime. The Court stuck to its distinction between customary and treaty law. It has never ruled on the government's argument that GCIV does not apply *de jure* in the West Bank, and has also refused to hold that all the provisions of the Convention have become part of customary law.[256] Nevertheless, the Court regularly relies on various articles in the Geneva Convention, sometimes referring to the government's commitment to abide by the Convention's humanitarian provisions.[257] On the other hand, the Court has ruled time and again that the Hague Regulations apply in the West Bank, and that as customary law they are enforceable in Israel's domestic courts. It has placed

253 See the cases in Kretzmer and Ronen (n 57) 64-68.
254 *Jami'yat Iskan* case (n 165) para 10.
255 *Gaza Coast* case (n 136). para 3.
256 HCJ 2690/09 *Yesh Din v IDF Commander in the West Bank* [28 March 2010].
257 Kretzmer and Ronen (n 57) 70-72.

the emphasis on Article 43 of the Regulations that defines the primary obligation of an occupying power to restore and maintain public order and public life in the occupied territory. The Court stated that this article is "a quasi-constitutional framework provision that sets out the general framework for the way the duties and powers of the military commander must be exercised in occupied territory".[258] As mentioned above, reliance on the Hague Regulations as binding law necessarily implies that the West Bank is occupied territory, as defined in Article 42 of the Regulations.

6.2 Nature of Court's Review

How has the Court exercised its jurisdiction over petitions challenging government policies, practices and actions in the Occupied Territories? This question is addressed in my book, *The Occupation of Justice*.[259] In the present monograph I shall confine my remarks to the main features of the Court's record in these petitions.

1. The Court has rarely been prepared to rule that policies or practices of the authorities are unlawful, even when there are cogent arguments that these policies or practices are incompatible with international law.[260] Two main examples of this aspect of the Court's jurisprudence are the Court's decision that despite the clear language of Article 49, paragraph 1, of GCIV,[261] deportation of individual protected persons on security grounds is not unlawful;[262] and the Court's refusal to outlaw punitive demolition of houses.[263]

258 *Yesh Din (Quarries)* case (n 165) para 8.

259 *The Occupation of Justice: The Supreme Court of Israel and the Occupied Territories.* The first edition, of which I was the sole author, was published in 2002 by SUNY Press. The second edition, published by OUP in 2021 (n 57), was an expanded edition written together with Yaël Ronen.

260 The one exception is the decision in HCJ 3799/02 *Adalah v Officer Commanding Central Command* [2005] PD 60(3) 67, in which the Court ruled that the practice of asking local Palestinians to warn a neighbour that the IDF has come to arrest him is unlawful.

261 Article 49(1) provides: "Individual or mass forcible transfers, as well as deportations of protected persons from occupied territory to the territory of the Occupying Power or to that of any other country, occupied or not, are prohibited, regardless of their motive."

262 Kretzmer and Ronen (n 57) 421-432.

263 ibid ch 18.

2. On the other hand, the Court has on occasion been prepared to intervene in the implementation of policies or practices on the basis of the concrete facts in a specific case.[264] They have usually done so on grounds of Israeli administrative law, namely that the specific decision is highly unreasonable, or that it does not meet the demands of proportionality.
3. In numerous cases Palestinians have been able to obtain a remedy, or a partial remedy, in what I have termed "the Court's shadow".[265] In these cases, judicial review has pressured the authorities to modify their approach in the individual case, to reach a settlement with the petitioner, or to accept a recommendation of the Court even if the Court has not ruled against them.[266]
4. When it comes to security arguments, the Court has generally displayed deference towards the authorities, although in rare cases it has intervened in security cases on the grounds of lack of proportionality.[267]
5. Although the Court has ruled that the military authorities in the West Bank are bound by the rules of customary international law relating to belligerent occupation, in recent years it has tended to shy away from international law and to assess cases on the basis of Israel's public law.[268]
6. In recent cases in which the Court has purported to rule on the basis of international law, its analysis has been based on misconceptions, total lack of understanding of the applicable norms or contrived interpretation of the international norms.[269]

The Court's decisions relating to establishment of settlements merit special attention. These decisions are discussed below.

264 Hence in a few cases the Court has intervened in the decision to demolish a house on the grounds that the sanction would be disproportionate in the specific case. ibid 401-404.

265 ibid 508-510.

266 ibid 491-495.

267 See, eg, HCJ 2056/04 *Beit Surik v Government of Israel* [2004] PD 58(5) 807.

268 Tamar Hostovsky Brandes, 'The Diminishing Status of International Law in the Decisions of the Israel Supreme Court Concerning the Occupied Territories' (2020) 18 *International Journal of Constitutional Law* 767.

269 A glaring example is the Court's judgment in *Abu Aram* case (n 98). And see the criticism of the case by Ben-Naftali and Diamond (n 98).

6.3 Judicial Mechanisms to Legitimize Government Practices

One of the striking and, one must say, most disturbing features of the approach of Israel's authorities to the legal status of the West Bank, has been the clear disparity between the unambiguous jurisprudence of the Supreme Court and the attitude of the executive branch of government. When defending government actions in the West Bank before the Supreme Court government counsel have consistently relied on the customary international law of belligerent occupation. Outside the courtroom, in presenting Israel's position on the status of the West Bank, government spokespersons have either simply ignored the Court's jurisprudence, or have presented it in a misleading fashion. Examples of the former attitude is the brief submitted to the International Criminal Court in September 2024;[270] an example of the latter attitude is the Memorandum of the Attorney General published before the pre-trial court of the ICC considered the request of the ICC prosecutor for a ruling on her decision to open an investigation into the "situation in Palestine".[271] In that Memorandum the Attorney General cites one decision of the Supreme Court as authority for the view that the law of belligerent occupation only applies *de facto* in the West Bank because of the State's policy to apply that law. This was totally misleading (if not worse than that), since the authority cited was a judgment handed down early on in the development of the Court's jurisprudence, at a time when the Court was still ruling on the basis of the "pragmatic approach" mentioned above. Since that judgment there have been many judgments of the Supreme Court applying the Hague Regulations and stating quite categorically that the West Bank is subject to a regime of belligerent occupation. All these decisions are ignored in the Attorney General's Memorandum.[272]

270 ICC, *Public Redacted Version of "Israel's challenge to the jurisdiction of the Court pursuant to article 19(2) of the Rome Statute"*, ICC-01/18-354-AnxII-Cor 04-10-2024 1/44 PT, paras 80-84, 114-118.

271 *The International Criminal Court's Lack of Jurisdiction* (n 159).

272 The Attorney General's memorandum is misleading in another way. The Attorney General states that Israel "applies the humanitarian provisions of the international law of occupation" (despite its principled position that they do not apply *de jure*). The term "the humanitarian provisions of the international law of occupation" obviously refers to the government's declaration that although GCIV does not formally apply in the West Bank, the IDF would comply with its humanitarian provisions. That declaration refers to GCIV and not to the Hague Regulations. The Attorney General's statement created the impression that it is only the humanitarian norms of occupation that the government applies, even though it is of the opinion that they

Despite the view of government spokespersons, the Court has not departed from its formal jurisprudence that the West Bank is subject to a regime of belligerent occupation. How has the Court coped with the disparity between this regime and government policies and practices? Or to put the question another way: how has the Court managed to grant explicit or implicit legitimization to government practices, even when these are incompatible with international law regime that applies in the West Bank? In our book, *The Occupation of Justice*, Yaël Ronen and I describe a number of judicial tools that have been used to achieve this result.[273]

6.3.1 Non-justiciability or lack of standing

One mechanism, described in more detail below, has been to rule that the specific issue before the Court is a political issue that is non-justiciable. As we shall see below, this tool has been employed in order to avoid ruling on the legality under international law of establishing settlements for citizens of the occupying power in the occupied territory. Another avoidance tool has been to rule that the petitioner lacks the standing to raise the question before the Court. Although rarely used, this tool was employed to avoid having to rule on the argument that using public land for an Israeli settlement is incompatible with customary international law as reflected in Article 55 of the Hague Regulations.[274]

---

do not bind Israel *de jure*. But this ignores the fact that the Supreme Court regularly relies on the Hague Regulations in order to justify infringements on the rights of the local population. A glaring example is the Court's reliance on the law of belligerent occupation in cases relating to construction of the Separation Barrier (Wall) in the West Bank. The Court justified taking and destroying private land and placing severe restrictions on the freedom of movement of Palestinians by citing various provisions in the Hague Regulations, as well as provisions in GCIV. Kretzmer and Ronen (n 57) ch 12, 233-272.

273 ibid 491-496.

274 HCJ 277/84 *Ghrayeb v Appeals Committee* [1986] PD 40(2) 57; HCJ 3125/98 *'Ayyad v IDF Commander in Judea and Samaria* [1999] PD 54(1) 913, opinion of Justice Mazza. These were remarkable decisions as the Supreme Court has widened the rules of standing before it, and has ruled that if there is no person with a personal and direct interest in the government action, when a serious legal question relating to the rule of law arises anyone has standing to bring the question before the Court: HCJ 511/80 *Gali v Haifa District Planning Committee* [1981] PD 35(4) 477; HCJ 852/86 *Aloni v Minister of Justice* [1987] PD 41(2) 1.

6.3.2 Distinction between customary and treaty law

Another mechanism has been to resort to the distinction between customary and treaty law, and to hold that the legality or illegality of the specific practice before the Court is determined by a provision in a treaty that cannot be enforced by the Court. This was the approach of the Court in a major case relating to deportation of a protected person, which is prohibited under Article 49, para. 1, of the GCIV. In the *Qawasmi* case, the majority on the Court held that the absolute prohibition on deportations is not part of customary international law, and that therefore it cannot be enforced by the Court.[275] In the first cases dealing with settlements, the Court held that the prohibition in Article 49 para. 6 of GCIV, that prohibits the occupying power from transferring part of its civilian population into the occupied territory, is not part of customary law.[276]

6.3.3 Convoluted interpretation of international law

Another tactic has been the convoluted and self-serving interpretation of international law. The prime example is the interpretation given to Article 49, para. 1 of GCIV. Despite its decision that the absolute prohibition on deportations in this provision is not part of customary law, in a few cases the Court interpreted this provision. Notwithstanding the clear language of the provision, including the stipulation that the prohibition on deportations of protected persons applies "whatever their motive", the Court held that the prohibition does not apply to deportation of individuals on security grounds.[277] The Court also held that deportation of over 400 persons who were selected for deportation solely for their alleged connection with a terrorist organization could not be regarded as a mass deportation.[278]

---

275 HCJ 698/80 *Qawasmi v Minister of Defence* [1980] PD 35(1) 617. In an imaginative judgment, the dissenting judge, Justice Haim Cohn, wrote that there is a general rule of customary international law that a state may not deport one of its own citizens and that this rule applies at all times, even in times of war. Justice Cohn opined that residents in occupied territory are to be regarded as citizens of that territory who may not be deported.

276 *Beth El* case (n 236); *Elon Moreh* case (n 151).

277 HCJ 97/79 *'Awad v Commander of Judea and Samaria* [1979] PD 33(3) 309; *Al-'Afou* case (n 109).

278 HCJ 5973/92 *Association for Civil Rights in Israel v Minister of Defence* [1993] PD 47(1) 267. Many years after this case, Dorit Beinisch, who as State Attorney at the

Another example of a contrived interpretation is the interpretation of Article 53 of GCIV that prohibits destruction of property in occupied territory "except where such destruction is rendered absolutely necessary by military operations". While this articles refers to "military operations" and not to protection of security that is mentioned in other articles of the Convention,[279] the Court has opined that this provision covers punitive demolition of the family home of a person involved in a terrorist attack.[280]

One of the more embarrassing interpretations of the Court relates to the prohibition on collective punishment in Article 33 of the Geneva Convention and Article 50 of the Hague Regulations.[281] In the first judgment relating to this issue, the Court dismissed the argument that demolishing the home of a family one of whose members was involved in a terrorist attack is a form of collective punishment, even when the family members were not involved in the attack and were not even aware of the activities of the family member. The Court stated:

> The object of Regulation 119 [the provision in local law that allows for house punitive house demolitions, DK] is "to achieve a deterrent effect" and this effect, by its very nature, must apply not only to the terrorist himself but also to those surrounding him, [and] certainly the members of his family who live with him. He must know that his heinous acts will not only harm him, but that they are likely to bring great suffering to his family.[282]

---

time had refused to defend the deportation in court, and later became President of the Supreme Court, wrote explaining that the deportation was clearly a mass deportation that could not be defended. See Dorit Beinisch, 'The Legal Proceedings Connected with the Deportation to Lebanon of Hamas Activists in December 1992' *Roots in the Law* (Ministry of Justice 25 March 2019) <https://www.gov.il/he/pages/roots_1992> accessed 15 January 2025.

279 See art 5 ("security of the state" and "security of the Occupying Power"); art 62 ("imperative reasons of security"); art 64 ("a threat to the security of the occupying power"); art 78 ("imperative reasons of security").

280 HCJ 8091/14 *Hamoked, Centre for the Protection of the Individual v Minister of Defence* [31 December 2014]; HCJ 6745/15 *Abu Hashia v IDF Commander in Judea and Samaria* [1 December 2015] , partially dissenting judgment of Justice Rubinstein. For criticism of this interpretation see Kretzmer and Ronen (n 57) 381-382.

281 Art 33 expressly prohibits collective punishment, while art 50 of the Hague Convention prohibits inflicting a penalty on the population "on account of individuals for which they cannot be regarded as jointly and severally responsible."

282 HCJ 698/85 *Dajlas v IDF Commander in Judea and Samaria* [1986] PD 40(2) 42.

I have called this decision embarrassing, since what the Court was really saying was not that house demolition is not a form of collective punishment;[283] rather it was explaining why collective punishment may be required! While a few of the judges on the Court have disassociated themselves with this view and have castigated punitive house demolitions as a form of collective punishment,[284] the Court itself has never been prepared to reconsider its precedents on this issue. In fact, the Court went even further and in numerous judgments it held that a punitive house demolition is not a form of punishment at all, but rather a form of prevention.[285] The Court simply ignored the facts that the provision in the local law that allows for house demolitions appears in a section entitled "Miscellaneous penal provisions", and that the authorities had initially answered the criticism that house demolitions are a form of reprisal by stating that they are a punitive measure.[286] It also failed to distinguish between prevention, which aims to destroy the means that enable commission of a criminal act, and deterrence, which aims to affect the willingness of persons to commit such an act.[287]

6.3.4 Ignoring or refraining from considering international law

Another tool of the Court in coping with the disparity between the practices and policies of the government and international law, has been simply to ignore, or refuse to consider, arguments based on international law. Thus, for example, in the first few cases on punitive house demolitions the Court considered the issue as one of interpreting the local law, without considering the implications of international law on the actions of the

---

283 Paul Rabbat and Sigrid Mehring, 'Collective Punishment' in *Max Planck Encyclopedias of Public International Law* (2015): "Collective punishment is a form of sanction imposed on persons or a group of persons in response to a crime committed by one of them or a member of the group."

284 See the dissenting opinion of Justice Cheshin in HCJ 2006/97 *Ghanimat v Officer Commanding Central Command* [1997] PD 51(2) 651; dissenting opinion of Justice Mazuz in HCJ 8150/15 *Abu Jamal v Officer Commanding Home Front* [22 December 2015] ; dissenting opinion of Justice Karra in HCJ 6905/18 *Naji v Military Commander in the West Bank* [2 December 2018].

285 The decisions are presented in Kretzmer and Ronen (n 57) 388-389.

286 ibid 388.

287 ibid.

occupying power.[288] In answer to arguments based on international law the Court stated that international law had no relevance for the case since the commander rested his authority to demolish houses on a provision in the law that was in force when the occupation began.[289] The view that the obligations of an occupying power do not apply when it relies on local law in the occupied territory is clearly fallacious.[290]

A glaring case of the refusal to consider the arguments under international law that had been raised by the parties is the case, mentioned above, in which the government decided to deport 400 alleged members of two terrorist organizations to Lebanon.[291] The decision was clearly incompatible with Article 49 of GCIV, and also raised other questions of international law, amongst which was the deportation of persons to a foreign country without the consent of the government of that country. Yet, even though these questions were raised before the Court, they are conspicuous by their absence in the Court's decision. Ignoring the serious issues of international law, the Court based its judgment on the duty to afford a hearing to persons against whom a deportation order has been issued.[292] Obviously the very power to deport protected persons should have been considered before the issue of a hearing, since if the deportation was *ipse facto* unlawful, there was no need for a hearing.

Another case in which the Court simply refused to consider arguments relating to international law related to establishment of an Israeli university in the West Bank. Circumventing the Israeli law on higher education that requires the approval of the Council on Higher Education for establishment of a new university, the government established a university in the

288 See HCJ 434/79 *Sahwell v IDF Commander of Judea and Samaria* [1979] PD 34(1) 646; HCJ 22/81 *Hamed v IDF Commander in Judea and Samaria* [1981] PD 35(3)223; HCJ 274/82 *Hamamrah v Minister of Defence* [1982] PD 36(2) 755.

289 *Sahwell* case (n 288); HCJ 897/86 *Jaber v Officer Commanding Central Command* [1987] PD 41(2) 522.

290 This was explained by Theodor Meron, legal adviser to the Foreign Ministry, in a legal opinion relating to house demolitions dated 12 March 1968, available at <https://www.akevot.org.il/article/theodor-meron-opinion/#popup/ae4241ffd6c3dcdb3b1234175c136074>. Among other authorities, Meron pointed to the view in the Pictet Commentary on the Geneva Conventions which states clearly that "when penal legislation of the occupied territory conflicts with the provisions of the Convention, the Convention must prevail." And see Kretzmer and Ronen (n 57) 46-48.

291 *Association for Civil Rights* case (n 278).

292 ibid. The only other argument that the Court mentioned, and rejected, was that the deportation was a mass deportation. See above, n 278.

West Bank settlement Ariel by using a series of military orders promulgated by the military commander of the West Bank. The presidents of the universities in Israel submitted a petition challenging the establishment of the university, but they restricted their arguments to grounds of Israeli administrative law, entirely ignoring the question of whether establishment of a university in occupied territory for the citizens of the occupying power is compatible with the obligations of an occupying power under international law. When an application was submitted by a third party that sought to bring the issues of international law before the Court, the Court dismissed the application to join the proceedings on the grounds that dealing with the applicant's arguments would unduly widen the legal issue before the Court.[293] The Court subsequently upheld the decision to establish the university without considering its legality under international law.[294]

6.3.5 Diluting the interests of the local population

Under international law the military commander in occupied territory is meant to exercise his powers for one or both of two considerations: his military needs and the interests of the local population. This is the way Justice Barak put the matter in a leading case:

> The powers and authority of the military commander are derived from the rules of public international law that deal with belligerent occupation... The considerations of the military commander are, on the one hand, ensuring his security interests in the [occupied] area, and, on the other hand, ensuring the interests of the civilian population in the area. Both of these considerations are directed towards the [occupied] area itself. The commander is not allowed to consider the national, economic or social interests of his own state, to the extent that they do not have implications for his security interests in the area or the interests of the local population. Even military needs are his military needs in the area, and not national security interests in the wide sense. An area subject to belligerent occupation is not a field open to economic or other exploitation.[295]

293 HCJ 6168/12 *Hebrew University of Jerusalem v Council for Higher Education in Judea and Samaria* [24 December 2013], para 30.

294 ibid.

295 *Jami'yat Iskan* case (n 165) para 10.

Justice Barak's dictum is an impeccable statement of the powers of a military commander in occupied territory. But how has the Court implemented this vision of the law in practice? The answer revolves first and foremost around the meaning of "ensuring the interests of the civilian population in the area". Two issues have been addressed by the Court: 1. Who is included amongst the civilian population in the area? 2. How does one assess "interests of the civilian population"?

In an early case the Court held that Israeli settlers in the area are included in the civilian population, and that the military commander can therefore consider their interests when he exercises his powers.[296] This view was repeated in a number of cases.[297] In the *Ziada* case Justice Joubran went as far as to state that since they are part of the local population, the military commander may expropriate private land for the benefit of Israeli settlers who live in the West Bank.[298] This statement stands in stark contradiction to the consistent view of the government's legal advisers, first reflected in a 1980 legal opinion of the Attorney General.[299] An application was submitted requesting a further hearing of the *Ziada* case. Although the President of the Court, Justice Hayut, dismissed the application on the grounds that Justice Joubran's dictum had not determined the outcome in the case, she

296 *Electricity Co (No 1)* case (n 121).

297 See, eg, HCJ 9717/03 *Na'aleh v Supreme Planning Commission in Judea and Samaria* [2004] PD 58(6) 97, in which Israeli settlers challenged the decision to locate a stone quarry near their settlement. They argued, inter alia, that establishing such as quarry was not for the good of the local population and was therefore incompatible with art 55 of the Hague Regulations that restricts the use by the occupying power of public property. The Court repeated the view that the settlers are part of the local population and since stone from the quarry would be used in Israeli settlements the quarry was being established for the good of the local population.

298 *Ziada case* (n 298). But see n 306, below.

299 In his letter to the Prime Minister dated 12 May 1980, the Attorney General expressed the view that land may not be expropriated unless it done so for the good of the local population, and that the view that settlers are included in the local population is highly problematical: <https://search.archives.gov.il/search/0b071706808b9f90> [in Hebrew] accessed 15 January 2025. And see letter of Senior Adviser to the Attorney General, dated 8 November 2017, in which he refers to "the traditional legal position of many years' standing that expropriating land for public purposes which serves Israeli settlement is only possible when the matter also serves the Palestinian population." Letter from Gil Limon, Senior Assistant to the Attorney General, 8 November 2017 <https://peacenow.org.il/wp-content/uploads/2017/11/Mendelblit_Opinion-confiscation-081117.pdf> [in Hebrew] accessed 15 January 2025.

admitted that the dictum "contradicts previous rulings and is both new and problematic".[300]

The legal problem that arises in relation to the status of Israeli settlers derives from the difference between the Hague Regulations and GCIV. While GCIV relates first and foremost to "protected persons", who do not include nationals of the occupying power,[301] the Hague Regulations refer simply to "inhabitants" of the occupied territory, thus opening the way for the claim that all inhabitants, including Israeli settlers, are protected under the Hague Regulations.[302] Yaël Ronen and I have exposed the weakness of this view, which undermines the special protection given under the laws of war in general, and the law of belligerent occupation in particular, to civilians of the enemy.[303]

In the *Regularization Law* case, Chief Justice Hayut regarded the local population as the population of "protected persons", as this term is defined in Article 4 of GCIV.[304] Chief Justice Hayut held that since private land in the West Bank may only be expropriated for a "public need", land of Palestinians could not be expropriated for the sole purpose of Israeli settlements. Seemingly, this ended the debate on the settlers as part of the local population.

The problem is that even without including the settlers as part of the local population for the purposes of the Hague Regulations, the Supreme Court has extended special protection to the settlers. It has done so by holding that the military commander is duty bound to protect the settlers' rights enshrined in Israel's constitutional law, even when this entails restricting

300 FHHCJ 9367/17 *Ziada v IDF Commander in the West Bank* [30 May 2018] para 7. Immediately after the original decision in this case, and before the decision of the President in the application for a further hearing, the Attorney General relied on Justice Joubran's dictum in a legal opinion allowing expropriation of private land to build an access road to an Israeli settlement: Letter from Gil Limon (n 299).

301 Art 4 of GCIV.

302 Ariel Erlich, 'Contrary to Past Precedents, "and is Both Novel, and Problematic": on Protecting the Property of "Protected Persons" Following the Judgment in HCJ 794/17 Ziada v. Commander of the IDF' (2018) 84 *Mivzakei Psika* 4 [in Hebrew].

303 Kretzmer and Ronen (n 57) 219-222. In his letter dated 12 May 1980 (n 299) the Attorney General presented the arguments for and against relating to the Israeli settlers as part of the local population for the purposes of the Hague Regulations.

304 HCJ 1308/17 *Silwad Local Council v The Knesset* [9 June 2020] para 33: "In dealing with the laws of belligerent occupation that apply in the [West Bank] and the protection which those laws grant to the inhabitants of the area, this Court has related to these inhabitants as "protected persons" as this term is defined in Article 4 of the Fourth Geneva Convention...".

the rights of the Palestinian residents of the area. In other words, the Court has held that the commander has a duty under Israeli constitutional law that empowers him to curtail the rights of Palestinians protected under the international law of belligerent occupation.[305] Hence Israeli settlers may even have stronger rights than those that the Palestinians enjoy as "protected persons". This prompted Justice Joubran to declare:

> Palestinian residents of the Area are not like any other group of individuals who are subject to the acts of this or that administrative authority. They are protected persons according to international law, who are entitled as such to special protection in a wide range of fields, including the sphere of private property.... Despite these provisions the protected persons are in an inherently inferior position to that of the Israeli settlers in the Area, who are full and equal citizens in the State of Israel.[306]

Turning now to the second issue – assessing the "interests of the local population" – the Court has seriously undermined the limits inherent in this duty of the military commander in three ways. In the first place, with one notable exception, the Court has examined the interests of the local population in a manner that is divorced from their vulnerable situation as a population subject to occupation. Secondly, and this is probably more significant, as emphasized by Chief Justice Hayut when she referred to illegality of expropriating land for the *sole* purpose of Israeli settlements, interests other than those of the local population may be considered, provided they are not the sole interests. Finally, there is no need to prove that the interests of the local population were in fact considered in the decision-making process. It is sufficient to show when the case comes to

---

305 HCJ 7957/04 *Mara'abe v Prime Minister of Israel* [2005] PD 60(2) 477, para 21. In listing the sources of the military commander's powers to seize property to build the separation barrier in the West Bank the Court mentioned the duty of the military commander to protect the rights of Israeli settlers protected in the *Basic Law: Human Dignity and Liberty* (1992). For other cases taking this line see Kretzmer and Ronen (n 57) 105-109.

306 *Ziada* case (n 298) para 115. Justice Joubran mentioned the special duties of the military commander towards "protected persons". He was fearful lest the resort to human rights norms of equality serves to undermine the special protection to which the inhabitants of the occupied territory are entitled under the law of belligerent occupation. On the potential deleterious effect of resorting to human rights norms in occupied territory see Aeyal Gross, 'Human Proportions: Are Human Rights the Emperor's New Clothes of the International Law of Occupation?' (2007) 18 *European Journal of International Law* 1.

court that the challenged decision will benefit the local population, even indirectly.

Let me start with the notable exception that shows the path that could have been taken. The *Electricity Corporation of the Jerusalem District* case concerned the decision of the Israeli Minister of Energy and the military commander in the West Bank to revoke the concession of the Palestinian electricity company to supply electricity in East Jerusalem and in parts of the West Bank, and to grant the right to supply electricity to the government Israel Electricity Corporation. Under Israel's domestic legal system, Israeli law applies in East Jerusalem and the Court found that the Minister's decision, based as it was on legitimate political grounds, was lawful. However, when it came to the military commander's decision, the question became whether the decision was in the interests of the local population. Justice Kahan held that it was not sufficient to show that the Israeli corporation could supply electricity more efficiently. He explained:

> When the Area came under the control of the commander of the Area, electricity was supplied by the petitioner, which is a local company. The result of using the option [to end the concession] will be that supply and distribution of electricity will be entirely in the hands of bodies outside the area, and given the importance of electricity in maintaining regular life of the public, this change has implications that go beyond the economic and technical aspects of the matter.[307]

As can be seen, Justice Kahan did not regard the test for assessing the interests of the local population solely in material terms; he included their interests as a population in occupied territory that at some future time will be free of the occupation. Such interests have not been considered in other cases, which have dealt mainly with building highways. The Court has simply stressed the advantages to the local population of new highways.[308]

A case in point is the case mentioned above in which Justice Barak laid down the principles that should guide the military commander in exercising his powers.[309] This case dealt with a plan to build a highway in the West Bank that would connect the main Tel Aviv-Jerusalem highway

307 HCJ 351/80 *Electricity Corporation of Jerusalem District v Minister of Energy and Infrastructure* [1981] PD 35(2) 673, para 13.

308 *Jami'yat Iskan* case (n 165); *Electricity Co (No 1)* case (n 121); HCJ 202/81 *Tabeeb v Minister of Defence* [1981] PD 36(2) 622; HCJ 6592/94 *Hebron Municipality v Minister of Defence* [1996] PD 50(2) 617.

309 *Jami'yat Iskan* case (n 165).

to northern Jerusalem. The highway had long been planned by Israeli decision-makers and planning bodies and when the plan was completed it was also approved by the Supreme Planning Council of the military government in the West Bank.[310] The military commander subsequently expropriated private land of Palestinians in the West Bank that was to be used for part of the project. There was no evidence that during the planning process serious consideration had been given to the interests of the local inhabitants in a massive highway that would pass through their territory. Nevertheless, when the case came to court the authorities produced an opinion of an Israeli expert who opined that there had been a huge growth in the number of vehicles in the West Bank and that Palestinian drivers would therefore benefit from the project. The Court conceded that Israeli drivers would benefit from the highway, but the mere fact that Palestinian drivers would benefit too was sufficient for the Court to hold that the highway would be built for the interests of the local population. The Court did not consider whether the interests of the local population should be the dominant consideration (clearly in this case they were not), nor whether the supposed interests of some Palestinian drivers were sufficient to satisfy the demand that the military commander act in the interests of the local population. What interest did the mainly agricultural Palestinian communities in the area have in a massive highway being built in vicinity of their homes and fields that would serve the interests of the residents of the occupying power? The Palestinians were not party to the decision to build the highway and even though they had the right to submit objections to the plan, those objections would be considered by a decision-making body comprised only of Israelis. Had the Court followed the path of Justice Kahan in the *Electricity Corporation* case mentioned above, it would have had to examine wider interests of the local population, and not only the advantages of the highway for some Palestinian car owners. Had the Court done so it would not have found it that easy to accept that the highway was being built in the interests of the local Palestinian population.

The dictum of Justice Barak on the duties of the military commander creates the impression that the main object of any decision of the commander must be his military interests or the interests of the local population.

310 For a detailed description of the planning process for this highway and the manipulative way in which the issue was presented see David Kretzmer and Gershom Gorenberg, 'Politics, Law and the Judicial Process: The Case of the High Court and the Territories' (2016) 17 *Mishpat Umimshal* 249 [in Hebrew].

But as the actual decision in the case in which Justice Barak made the pronouncement reveals, the Court has held otherwise: it is sufficient that the authorities can point to some advantage to Palestinian residents in order for the Court to accept that the decision was in the interests of the local population. This is the case even if their interests were not actually seriously considered during the decision-making process, or if the "national, economic or social interests" of Israel were the dominant factor in the decision. Hence, in the VAT case, the Court held that imposing VAT (value added tax) in the occupied territories to correspond with its imposition in Israel, was in the interests of the local population.[311] The reason given was that there were at the time open borders between Israel and the West Bank and Gaza, and that if the tax was not imposed in those territories, the authorities would have had to close the borders. This would not have been in the interests of the local population. In another case the Court went even further and opined that allowing Israeli corporations to work quarries in the West Bank for stone that was to be used in Israel was in the interests of the local population since the quarries provided employment for local Palestinian residents.[312] According to this logic Israeli settlements were in the interests of the local population since most of the workers employed in building them were Palestinian residents of the West Bank.[313]

---

311 HCJ 69/81 *Abu 'Itta v IDF Commander in Judea and Samaria* [1983] PD 37(2) 197.

312 *Yesh Din (Quarries)* case (n 165). In fairness it must be pointed out that the petition in this case was dismissed on procedural grounds and that this dictum of the Court was added as an afterthought that was not the basis for the Court's judgment.

313 Matthew Vickery, *Employing the Enemy: The Story of Palestinian Labourers on Israeli Settlements* (Zed Books 2017).

Chapter 7: The Politics of Occupation

7.1 Immediate Aftermath of the June 1967 War

Upon taking control over the West Bank the military commander issued a proclamation that all governmental authority was now in his hands. This was in conformity with the practice in international law that the regime in occupied territory is essentially a military regime.[314] As the occupying power does not gain sovereignty in the occupied territory[315] the idea is that the non-political military should be responsible for ruling the area on a temporary basis, until local forces can assume most of the governmental functions, or until a political settlement to end the occupation is reached.

In the leading judgment mentioned above Justice Barak stressed that the military commander in occupied territory must act only for his military interests or in the interests of the local population, and that he may not even consider "the national, economic or social interests" of his own state.[316] While an accurate statement of the law, it was at the time, and continues to this day, to be totally divorced from the reality of the exercise of governmental power in the occupied territories. The military commander is an organ of the Israeli executive branch of government. As such he is bound to implement government policies. Despite the military orders and proclamations promulgated when the IDF gained control over the West Bank and Gaza, from the very start of the occupation the policies and practices to be followed by the military commanders were set by various political decision-making bodies. These included a number of Cabinet committees and a coordinating committee of the directors general of government ministries.[317]

The most important figure in suggesting, promoting, and implementing government policy during the first seven years of the occupation was the

314 Dinstein (n 1) 65: "With or without a structured administration, the government of an occupied territory is military *per definitionem*."

315 ibid 58-60. Dinstein cites Oppenheim who wrote that "there is not an atom of sovereignty in the authority of the Occupying Power".

316 *Jami'yat Iskan* case (n 165).

317 Shefer Raviv (n 64).

charismatic and dominant Minister of Defence, Moshe Dayan.[318] Dayan was the person who selected the officers charged with the day-to-day running of the occupation and who gave them instructions on which policies and practices to follow. The military commander was simply in charge of implementing the policies and practices decided by Dayan, generally with the approval of the Cabinet or the relevant Cabinet committee.[319] When new legislation was needed the military commander used his formal authority to promulgate military orders.

One may expect military commanders to base their decisions and actions solely on their military needs and the interests of the population under their control. However, when it comes to the political bodies of the occupying power, such an expectation is not realistic. Apart from their own domestic political interests, the foremost considerations of such bodies are going to be their perception of the security, national, economic, political and social interests of their own country, and not the narrow military needs of the military commander or the interests of the local population. To the extent that the interests of the local population in the occupied territory are considered they will be a factor to be taken into account in assessing the interests of the occupying power.

Omri Shefer Raviv's meticulous study of the first two years of the occupation reveals that the policies and practices in the occupied territory were indeed based on the government's perception of Israel's long-term interests.[320] How were these interests perceived?

In a speech he delivered in November 1967, Prime Minister Levi Eshkol described how he viewed Israel's victory in the June 1967 War. In his picturesque language, Eshkol stated that in that war Israel had received a wonderful dowry. The problem was that it did not want the bride.[321] This view informed Israeli policy in the newly occupied territories in the first year of Israel's control over the West Bank and Gaza.[322] Policies were adopted that were designed to encourage the bride (namely, the Palestini-

318 ibid 15.
319 ibid 61-95.
320 ibid.
321 Raz (n 63) 39.
322 Omri Shefer Raviv 'Israeli Emigration Policies in the Gaza Strip: Crafting Demography and Forming Control in the Aftermath of the 1967 War' (2021) 57 *Middle Eastern Studies* 342; Omri Shefer Raviv 'Science and Politics in Demographic Planning: The Case of Encouraging Arab Emigration from the Territories' (Institute for National Security Studies February 2024) <https://www.inss.org.il/he/wp-content/uploads/sites/2/2024/06/%D7%A2%D7%9E%D7%A8%D7%99-%D7%A9%D7%A

ans) to move from Gaza to the West Bank, and to emigrate from both of these territories, while at the same time trying to create the conditions for long-term control over the dowry (namely, the land).

The attempt to ease what Zionists saw as the "demographic problem", namely the danger that Jews would become a minority in the Jewish state, was incompatible with the desire to maintain long-term control over the land. Encouraging emigration required making things difficult for the local population, especially when it came to economic development and chances of gainful employment; maintaining long-term control over the occupied territories demanded creating decent economic conditions so that the local population would have much to lose by opposing the occupation.

At first there were some members of the government who favoured a future agreement under which Israel would relinquish control over most of the West Bank. But after the August 1967 Khartoum summit of the Arab League, in which Israel's neighbours declared that there would be no negotiations, no peace and no recognition of Israel,[323] consensus was reached that Israel should prepare for long-term control over the West Bank and Gaza. This policy was strongly promoted by Minister of Defence Moshe Dayan, who was convinced that mainly for security reasons, but also because of the Jewish people's historic attachment to the land, Israel should maintain permanent control over the West Bank.[324] Dayan was of the opinion that if Israel would allow the Palestinians control over their daily lives, with as little interference as possible by the Israeli authorities, a *modus vivendi* could be created that would allow Israel to maintain a permanent military presence in the West Bank.

Dayan was a person of contradictions. Hence, while he was totally aware of the fundamental reasons for Palestinian antagonism towards the Jewish state,[325] he nevertheless thought that national aspirations and deeply-held feelings of historic injustice could be contained by paternalistic economic

---

4%D7%A8%D6%BE%D7%A8%D7%91%D7%99%D7%91.pdf> accessed 15 January 2025.

323 'Fourth Arab Summit, Resolution', (Khartoum 1 September 1967) <https://www.palquest.org/en/historictext/9615/fourth-arab-summit-resolutions> accessed 15 January 2025.

324 Shafer Raviv (n 64) 102-109.

325 In a remarkable eulogy for a kibbutz security officer murdered by Palestinians who had crossed the armistice line between Israel and Gaza, Dayan, who at the time (1956) was the IDF Chief of Staff, referred to frequent attacks by Palestinians from Gaza, and posed the following question: "Why should we blame them for their burning hatred for us? For eight years they have been dwelling in Gaza's refugee camps, as before their eyes we have transformed the land and the villages in

and social policies. He was neither the first, nor the last, person who imagined that by considered use of force and benevolent economics, a people could permanently be denied the right to self-determination.

It did not take long for the decision-makers to realize that attempts to encourage emigration of Palestinians had failed. The attempts were abandoned and the policy turned to making Israel's presence in the West Bank permanent without formally annexing the territory. One of the main supporters of this policy was Prime Minister Levi Eshkol. Eshkol was apparently obsessed with the "demographic issue", but at the same time he became convinced that for security reasons Israel had to maintain long-term military control over the West Bank.[326] He was shrewd enough to realise that Israel's attempts to encourage Palestinian emigration were doomed to fail, but was concerned that if Israel relinquished control over any part of the West Bank there would be a large return of Palestinian refugees to the territory, thus making the Jews a clear minority in the territory "from the river to the sea".[327]

To summarize: from very soon after the occupation began in 1967, political decision-makers based the policies in the West Bank on their perception that Israel's security interests required maintaining permanent control over the territory. The military commander's obligations to consider only his military needs and the interests of the local population were largely

---

which they and their forefathers had dwelled into our own property." Chemi Shalev, 'Moshe Dayan's Enduring Eulogy: "This if the Fate of our Generation"' *Ha'aretz* (20 July 2014) <https://www.haaretz.com/2014-07-20/ty-article/.premium/moshe-dayans-enduring-gaza-eulogy-this-is-the-fate-of-our-generation/0000017f-dc5b-df9c-a17f-fe5bf1150000?lts=1728311567751> accessed 15 January 2025. The full text of the eulogy is available on the IDF webpage devoted to Dayan: <https://www.idf.il/%D7%A8%D7%90%D7%A9%D7%99-%D7%94%D7%9E%D7%98%D7%94-%D7%94%D7%9B%D7%9C%D7%9C%D7%99/%D7%94%D7%A8%D7%9E%D7%98%D7%9B-%D7%9C-%D7%94-4/%D7%93%D7%91%D7%A8%D7%99-%D7%94%D7%A8%D7%9E%D7%98%D7%9B-%D7%9C/30-4-1956-%D7%A8%D7%90-%D7%9C-%D7%9E%D7%A9%D7%94-%D7%93%D7%99%D7%99%D7%9F-%D7%9E%D7%A1%D7%A4%D7%99%D7%93-%D7%90%D7%AA-%D7%A8%D7%95%D7%A2%D7%99-%D7%A8%D7%95%D7%98%D7%91%D7%A8%D7%92-%D7%96-%D7%9C/> accessed 15 January 2025.

326 Shefer-Raviv (n 64) 45-46.

327 ibid. Shefer-Raviv writes about a December 1967 meeting of Eshkol with the IDF General Staff in which all officers were of the view that for security reasons Israel must maintain control over the West Bank. Only the Chief of Staff, Yitzchak Rabin, thought that Israel could allow Palestinian autonomy in the northern part of the West Bank. Eshkol's remarks on the Palestinian immigration that would take place were made in response to Rabin's view.

irrelevant, given that policy and practices in the occupied territories were determined by the Cabinet and other political decision-making bodies, and that military officers were bound to implement government policy.

7.2 Beginnings of the Settlement Policy

The most important manifestation of the decision to maintain permanent control over the West Bank is the establishment there of Israeli settlements.[328] This policy began soon after the June 1967 War, when members of families who had lived in Jewish settlements that had been conquered and destroyed by Jordanian forces in 1948 pressured the government to allow them to return to the Gush Etzion area near Jerusalem and to establish settlements in place of those that had been destroyed.

It was in this context that Prime Minister Eshkol requested a legal opinion on the legality of establishing Israeli settlements in the West Bank. We know, however, that Theodor Meron's opinion that establishment of such settlements would be incompatible with international law did not deter the government from proceeding with settlements. The only apparent effect of Meron's opinion was the decision that the first settlements established in the Jordan valley were *Nachal* settlements, namely agricultural settlements that were manned by soldiers as part of their compulsory military service.[329]

Under the Labour government that was in power until 1977, the settlement policy allowed for massive settlement in East Jerusalem that had been annexed under Israeli domestic law, and for settlements in the West Bank close to the Green Line, and in the Jordan valley. There was one notable

328 Soon after the settlement policy in the occupied territories was initiated Dayan stated: 'I regard settlement as the most important thing and the factor that has the greatest weight in creating political facts, on the basis of the assumption - as the Prime Minister has also stated - that we will not leave a place in which we have established a settlement or outpost. Therefore, in determining the map and in determining our desire for a new map, I see settlement as the most symbolic factor and the one that will most bind us ourselves', cited in Reuven Pedatzur, *The Triumph of Embarrassment, Israel and the Territories After the Six-Day War* (Yad Tabenkin 1996) 161 [in Hebrew].

329 The Nahal movement was founded in the early years of the state when the ethos of agricultural work and the kibbutz movement were strong. Soldiers who joined Nahal combined agricultural work (often in new agricultural settlements close to the border) and military service.

exception: the establishment of the Kiryat Arba settlement on the outskirts of the largest West Bank city, Hebron.[330]

While nationalistic sentiments and emotional attachment to the Land of the Bible played a part in the settlement policy, under the Labour government the main considerations were security and strategic considerations, based on the desire to maintain an Israeli presence in the areas surrounding Jerusalem and in the Jordan valley, which was meant to be Israel's permanent security border. There was wide consensus that Israel should maintain a permanent military presence in the West Bank; at the same time there was also agreement that there should not be settlements near the main Palestinian cities and towns. According to one view, advanced by Yigal Alon,[331] Israel should aim for an agreement with Jordan under which Jordan would gain civilian control over the populated Palestinian areas; under the view of Moshe Dayan, the Palestinians should have some form of autonomy in those areas. There were bitter disputes amongst the parties that comprised the Labour Alignment[332]over the issue of settlements, with some pushing for massive expansion of the settlements and others objecting to more settlements.[333]

This all changed when Menachem Begin became prime minister in 1977. His party, the Likud party, believed in the right of Jews to settle in all parts of the historic Land of Israel and was committed to advancing a policy of settlement in the West Bank.[334] This policy, which was initiated in 1977

330 For full discussion of the settlement policy during the period 1967-1977 see Gershom Gorenberg (n 70); cf. Eldar and Zertal (n 245) 32, who write that establishment in April 1975 of the Ofra settlement on the Ramallah-Nablus highway, was the first breach in the obstacle to establishing settlements in the vicinity of Palestinian cities.

331 Alon was deputy prime minister in Levi Eshkol's government and later became foreign minister in the government headed by Yitzchak Rabin (1974-1977).

332 The Labour Alignment was comprised of three factions: the core Labour Party faction, a faction that had been part of the pro-settlement Achdut Avoda Party, and the Mapam Party that opposed new settlements in the West Bank. Even amongst members of the core Labour faction, there were some who were strong proponents of the settler movement.

333 The divisions came to a head after the government negotiated with supporters of the *Gush Emunim* settler group who had taken over the old Sebastia railway station, near the West Bank city Nablus. Under the agreement the people would leave Sebastia, but thirty families would be allowed to live in a nearby army camp. Within two to three months the government would discuss settlement policy: Gorenberg (n 70) ch 11; Eldar and Zertal (n 245) 41-45.

334 The Likud platform of 1977 declared that in all of the Land of Israel there will only be Israeli sovereignty. It stated: 'Settlement, both urban and rural, in all parts of

and continues in full force to the present day, has totally transformed the West Bank. At the time the Labour Party was defeated in the 1977 elections there were less than 10,000 Israelis settled in the West Bank (outside of Jerusalem).[335] At the end of 2023 there were over 500,000 settlers there.[336]

The settlement policy of Begin's government rested on the belief that Jews have a right to settle in all parts of the Land of Israel. At the same time the policy had another, more political, aim. The aim was not only to ensure permanent control over the West Bank but to create the conditions that would make it impossible to establish another state in that area.[337]

In considering the government's settlement policy it is important to point out that the military commander, who is supposed to make decisions based solely on his military need and the interests of the local population, had no hand in setting this policy, although he was required to take the steps necessary under the military law to facilitate its implementation. When the government decided to adopt a radical move of using public land for establishment of settlements, the military commander was not

---

the Land of Israel is the focal point of the Zionist effort to redeem the country, to maintain vital security areas and serves as a reservoir of strength and inspiration for the renewal of the pioneering spirit.' See <https://www.jewishvirtuallibrary.org/original-party-platform-of-the-likud-party> accessed 15 January 2025.

335 See Gorenberg (n 70) Location 6712 in digital edition. The exact numbers for the West Bank are not clear as the number of settlers in the occupied territories cited by various sources included settlers in the Golan Heights and the Sinai Peninsula. According to the figures published by the Peace Now movement in 1978 there were 7,800 settlers in the occupied territories: <https://peacenow.org.il/en/population-data-in-israel-and-in-the-west-bank> accessed 15 January 2025. At the same time, before it lost the elections the Labour Party government's Ministerial Committee on Settlement had approved plans for building 17 new settlements in the West Bank: Neve Gordon (n 68) 217.

336 According to a report by a settler group, based on the data of Israel's Central Bureau of Statistics, at the end of 2023 there were close to 520,000 Israeli settlers in the West Bank: *The Times of Israel* (12 February 2024) <https://www.timesofisrael.com/west-bank-settler-population-grew-by-nearly-3-in-2023-report/> accessed 19 January 2025 .

337 The settlement policy adopted by the Begin government was set out by Matityahu Drobles, head of the Settlement Division of the World Zionist Organisation. This plan stated that the objectives of the settlements were to "reduce to the minimum the possibility for the development of another Arab state in these regions" and to make it difficult for the local Palestinian population "to form a territorial continuity and political unity when it is fragmented by Jewish settlements." Matityahu Drobles, *Settlement in Judea and Samaria: Strategy, Policy and Planning* (WZO Settlement Division 1980) 3.

consulted whether this policy was compatible with his legal obligations as the governing authority in the West Bank.

7.3 Settlements: Legal Aspects

The international community has consistently taken the position that in establishing Israeli settlements in the West Bank, Israel violates international law. This is the position of the UN Security Council,[338] the International Court of Justice,[339] the ICRC,[340] the EU,[341] and the states parties to the Geneva Conventions.[342]

The opinion of the international community regarding the illegality of establishing settlements in occupied territory rests on Article 49(6) of GCIV that prohibits the occupying power from transferring part of its own civilian population into the occupied territory. It should be appreciated, however, that there are other cogent reasons for holding that establishment of settlements in occupied territory for citizens of the occupying power is incompatible with international law.[343] As we saw above, the Supreme Court of Israel has held that in using his powers the military commander in occupied territory must consider only one or both of two considerations: his military needs in the occupied territory, and the interests of the local population. While in two cases the Supreme Court held that establishment of three specific settlements could be justified on security grounds,[344] no

338 See, eg, UNSC Res 2334 (n 8) that reaffirms all the Council's previous resolutions on the matter.

339 *Wall* Advisory Opinion (n 82); Advisory Opinion, *Occupied Palestinian Territory* (n 9).

340 Maurer (n 122) 1506.

341 'EU condemns Israel latest move to expand illegal settlements in West Bank' *Middle East Monitor* (4 July 2024) <https://www.middleeastmonitor.com/20240704-eu-condemns-israel-latest-move-to-expand-illegal-settlements-in-west-bank/> accessed 15 January 2025.

342 Lanz, Max and Hoehne (n 164).

343 Benvenisti (n 1) 241; Antonio Cassese, 'Powers and Duties of an Occupant in Relation to Land and Natural Resources' in Emma Playfair (ed), *International Law and the Administration of Occupied Territories: Two Decades of Israeli Occupation of the West Bank and Gaza Strip* (OUP 1992) 419.

344 Kretzmer and Ronen (n 57) 197-201. I do not go into the question here if under international law it is possible to justify establishment of settlements in occupied territory on military or security grounds. As Theodor Meron stated in his opinion of September 1967 the prohibition on transferring civilians of the occupying power

concrete security grounds were cited for establishment of other settlements. The military commanders had no hand in the decision to establish settlements and so it is hard to see how they could be justified as serving the military needs of the commander.[345] There is also no possible way to argue that establishment of settlements was in the interests of the local population. On the contrary, the settlements have had a hugely deleterious effect on both individual and collective rights of the Palestinian inhabitants.[346]

In his legal opinion on the establishment of settlements, Theodor Meron mentioned restrictions on seizing land in occupied territory. The military commander is entitled to seize private land on a temporary basis for military purposes, but he does not have the power to expropriate land unless this is done for the benefit of the public under the local law in the occupied territory. Under Art 55 of the Hague Regulations the occupying power is a trustee of the public property. It is a usufructuary that may enjoy the fruits of public property but may not appropriate the property.

In the first cases in which settlements were established in the West Bank, the military commander issued orders seizing private land for military purposes. In two cases the Palestinian land-owners challenged the seizure of their land before the Supreme Court.[347] The Court held that under international law the military commander in occupied territory has the power to seize land on a temporary basis for military purposes.[348] It also accepted the argument that these particular settlements had been

into the occupied territory would seem to be absolute and not to allow an exception on security grounds.

345 In the *Elon Moreh* case (n 165) the Supreme Court held that since there was no military planning, while the commander had seized the land, ostensibly for military needs, following a political decision to establish a settlement, the seizure order was incompatible both with international law and Israeli administrative law.

346 See UN Human Rights Council, 'Report of the independent international factfinding mission to investigate the implications of the Israeli settlements on the civil, political, economic, social and cultural rights of the Palestinian people throughout the Occupied Palestinian Territory, including East Jerusalem' (7 February 2013) UN Doc A/HRC/22/63; Gordon (n 68) ch 5; B'tselem, 'By Hook and by Crook: Israeli Settlement Policy in the West Bank' (July 2010) <https://www.btselem.org/publications/summaries/201007_by_hook_and_by_crook> accessed 15 January 2025.

347 *Beth El* case (n 236); HCJ 258/79 *'Amerah v Minister of Defence* [1979] PD 34(1) 90.

348 The Court relied on Art 52 of the Hague Regulations that allows the military commander to requisition property for the needs of the occupying army. The Court held that while seemingly this article applies to movable property, experts on the law of occupation agree that the military commander has the power to requisition land for his military needs.

established at strategic places for military reasons. In the *Beth El* case, in reply to the argument that establishing a settlement is not compatible with the temporary nature of seizing, as opposed to expropriating land, the Court held that the settlements were temporary in the sense that they could remain only as long as Israel retained control over the area. The judgment in this case was delivered just as Israel had agreed in the peace agreement with Egypt to remove all its settlements in the Sinai Peninsula. Hence the judgment was not entirely removed from political reality. Even so, the idea that a settlement that is meant to be permanent is established on land that is ostensibly taken on a temporary basis is stretching the notion of temporariness beyond its accepted use.[349] As the Court later held, when an order is made for temporary use of property a time limit should be set for such use.[350]

The Court's approach on the temporariness issue changed in the *Elon Moreh* case, mentioned above. As we saw above, giving in to pressure by the *Gush Emunim* settler movement, the government had decided to establish a settlement in the West Bank area of Samaria. After the Cabinet Committee on settlement decided that the settlement would be established on the private land of a Palestinian, the military commander issued an order seizing the land for military needs. Significantly, the Minister of Defence, the Foreign Minister who had previously served as IDF Chief of Staff and as Minister of Defence, and the Deputy Prime Minister, himself a former IDF Chief of Staff, had opposed establishing the settlement, which, they claimed, could not be justified on military grounds. The Court held that the since the dominant reasons for the seizure order of the land had been political, rather than military, the order was invalid both under Israeli administrative law and international law. The Court added that since it had been provided with evidence that the prime minister had promised that the settlement would be permanent, its establishment was incompatible with international law. In the words of the Deputy President, Justice Moshe Landau:

> The decision to establish a settlement that is from the outset planned to remain in its place indefinitely - even beyond the duration of the military government established in Judea and Samaria - meets an insurmountable legal obstacle, since no military government may create in its area facts

349 Ben-Naftali, Sfard and Viterbo (n 1) 399.

350 HCJ 290/89 *Jouha v Military Commander in Judea and Samaria* [1989] PD 43(2) 116. Also see the dictum of Chief Justice Hayut in *Silwad* case, cited above in n 304.

> for its military needs that are designed *ab initio* to persist even after the end of the military rule in the area, when the fate of the area after the termination of the military rule is still not known.[351]

In other words, the Court's approach on the question of temporariness now rested on the intention behind the establishment of a settlement, and not on the possibility that the settlement might be removed in the future. If the intention was that the settlement should be permanent, private land seized on a temporary basis could not be used for the settlement, even if it was possible that at some time in the future a political decision could be taken to remove the settlement.

Justice Landau refrained from using the term "occupied territory" and provided no authority for the proposition he presented. It seems clear, however, that the "insurmountable legal obstacle" to which he was referring is the principle that a regime of belligerent occupation is by its very nature a temporary regime, with all that this implies as regards the powers of the military commander.[352] Hence the "legal obstacle" was not confined to the specific issue before the Court, namely the seizure of private land for a permanent settlement. Seemingly, as a general precept of the law of belligerent occupation, it has implications for all use by the military commander of his powers in the occupied territory. I return to this aspect of the *Elon Moreh* case below.

In the *Beth El* case, decided before the *Elon Moreh* case, it was argued that establishing a settlement in the West Bank is incompatible with Article 49(6) of GCIV. The Court held that Article 49(6) does not reflect customary international law and that the Court would therefore refrain from addressing the argument. At the same time Justice Landau added the following comment:

> I have more willingly reached the conclusion that this court should refrain from dealing with the problem of civilian settlement in occupied territory from the point of view of international law, since I know that it is in dispute between the Government of Israel and other governments and is likely to form part of the fateful international negotiations in which the Government of Israel is engaged. Any expression of opinion

351 *Elon Moreh* case (n 151) para 20.

352 See Ben-Naftali, Sfard and Viterbo (n 1) 11. In describing the tenets of a regime of belligerent occupation, Ben-Naftali writes: "This regime ...rests on three precepts: exceptionality, limited scope of powers, and temporary duration....the duration must be limited and it must not generate permanent effects."

> by this court in such a sensitive matter, which could only be made obiter would be neither here nor there, and it is better that matters that by their nature pertain to the international political plane should be dealt with only on that plane.[353]

In the *Elon Moreh* case, the Court was prepared to examine whether land on which a settlement was to be built and which was ostensibly taken for military purposes was indeed taken for such purposes. However, following its approach in the *Beth El* case, the Court was not prepared to consider the argument raised by the Palestinian petitioners that establishing settlements in the occupied territories is *per se* incompatible with international law.

The Court's decisions in the *Beth El* and *Elon Moreh* cases were to set the basis for the Court's approach to judicial review over the legality of settlements. While the Court is prepared to review whether land for a specific settlement was taken legally, it is not prepared to consider the argument that establishing a settlement in the West Bank for Israeli civilians is *per se* unlawful.

In the *Bargil* case the Peace Now movement submitted a petition to the Court challenging the settlement policy on numerous grounds, including the arguments under customary law. The Court refused to consider the arguments, holding that the dominant nature of the settlements issue is political, and that the issue is therefore non-justiciable.[354] One of the judges conceded that the petitioners had presented cogent legal arguments in their pleadings, but stated that they had laid a mine on the Court's doorstep, and that the Court would not step on the mine lest it destroy public trust in the Court.[355] Since the *Beth El*, *Elon Moreh* and *Bargil* judgments it has become the accepted jurisprudence of the Court that the legality of settlements is a political issue on which the Court will not deliver an opinion.[356]

One can appreciate why from a political point of view the Court wished to avoid ruling on the legality of establishing settlements in the West Bank. Not only is the issue a highly controversial issue in Israel itself, and one for which Israel has been severely censured by the UNSC and other

353 *Beth El* case (n 236). At the time the case was heard Israel was negotiating the terms of the peace agreement with Egypt. As mentioned above, under that agreement Israel eventually agreed to remove all the settlements that it had established in Sinai after 1967.

354 HCJ 4481/91 *Bargil v Government of Israel* [1993] PD 47(4) 210.

355 Justice Goldberg, ibid.

356 David Kretzmer, 'Settlements in the Supreme Court of Israel' (2017) 111 *AJIL Unbound* 41.

international bodies, but as Justice Landau explained in the *Beth El* case, the issue arose before the Court when establishing settlements was being considered in international negotiations.[357] The Court was not going to deliver a judgment that would have weakened the government's position in those negotiations.

Furthermore, the settlement policy was a major policy of the government that had come to power after the elections in 1977. It is highly unlikely that the government would have abandoned its settlement policy following a ruling of the Court that this policy is incompatible with international law. Even after the Court held that establishment of a specific planned settlement on private land was unlawful, there were calls in the political arena to enact legislation removing the jurisdiction of the Court to consider government actions in the occupied territories, or providing that establishment of settlements is lawful.[358]

The Court's refusal to rule on the legality of the settlements came under strain when the government decided to build a separation barrier in the West Bank. The legality of the barrier's route in occupied territory was considered by the International Court of Justice in its Advisory Opinion in the *Wall* case.[359] The ICJ opined that since the establishment of settlements for civilians of the occupying power is unlawful, determining the route of the separation barrier so as to include settlements on the western, Israeli, side of the barrier was unlawful too.[360]

357 In the *Beth El* case (n 236) the hearing took place whilst negotiations with Egypt were taking place; The *Bargil* case (n 354) was heard whilst negotiations that led to the Oslo Accords with the PLO were being taking place.

358 The various proposals are mentioned in para 15 of the Letter of the Attorney General dated 25 February 1980, available at <https://www.thelawfilm.com/inside/wp-content/uploads/2015/11/1980-02-25-%D7%99%D7%95%D7%A2%D7%9E%D7%A9-%D7%96%D7%9E%D7%99%D7%A8-%D7%97%D7%95%D7%95%D7%93-%D7%A2%D7%9C-%D7%94%D7%9E%D7%A2%D7%9E%D7%93-%D7%94%D7%9E%D7%A9%D7%A4%D7%98%D7%99-%D7%A9%D7%9C-%D7%99%D7%A9%D7%95%D7%91%D7%99%D7%9D-%D7%99%D7%A9%D7%A8%D7%90%D7%9C%D7%99%D7%9D-%D7%91%D7%99%D7%95%D7%A9.pdf> [in Hebrew] accessed 14 March 2025.

359 *Wall* Advisory Opinion (n 82).

360 Ibid. In para. 120 the Court concluded that Israeli settlements in the Occupied Palestinian Territories were established in breach of international law. In ruling that the route of the barrier was unlawful the Court stated that: 'the route chosen for the wall gives expression *in loco* to the illegal measures taken by Israel with regard to Jerusalem and the settlements.' (ibid, para 122).

Soon after the Advisory Opinion was published, the Supreme Court heard a case relating to a section of the barrier that surrounded a settlement in the West Bank, and that consequently placed severe restrictions on Palestinian communities in the area.[361] The petitioners argued that the Court should follow the line of the ICJ relating to the route of the barrier. The Court was faced with a real dilemma. Having refrained for over thirty-five years from ruling on the legality of establishing settlements in the West Bank, it was in no position to do so now. On the other hand, it was highly reluctant to cross swords with the ICJ that had held that establishment of settlements in the West Bank is unlawful. The Court manipulated its way out of this dilemma by ruling that the legality of the settlements is irrelevant in deciding on the legality of the separation barrier's route. According to the Court, even if the settlements are unlawful the military commander has the duty to protect the lives of the residents of those settlements, and the barrier's route could therefore be justified on security grounds.

The Court's reasoning is unconvincing.[362] The question in the case before the Court was not whether the military commander has a duty to protect the settlers' lives, but whether routing the barrier to include the settlements on its western, Israeli, side was a legitimate way of doing so, especially when this meant severely curtailing rights of Palestinians in the area. If the settlement was indeed unlawful, surely the rights of the Palestinian inhabitants of the area who were all living in perfectly lawful villages should have been preferred to those of the settlers. Hence the commander should have been forced to find other ways of protecting the settlers, such as removing the illegal settlement, or at the very least building a fence around the settlement itself.

The refusal of the Court to rule on the legality of settlements is a clear example of the political constraints on the Court, which is struggling to maintain public trust amongst a public that has become more and more nationalistic and less and less tolerant of liberal views over the years. Since the present government came to power at the end of 2022, it has mounted a concerted attack on the Court; the government's plan for change in the constitutional regime of the state involves executive control over the ap-

361 *Mara'abe* case (n 305).
362 Kretzmer and Ronen (n 57) 255-259.

pointment of judges and restrictions on the power of the Court to exercise judicial review over governmental actions and decisions.[363]

The Court's position on the settlements has compromised all its jurisprudence relating to the application of the law of belligerent occupation in the West Bank. The Court has left open the question of the settlements' legality, but it has catered to the interests of the settlers at the expense of the rights of Palestinian residents in many ways. First and foremost, while the Court does not allow taking of private land for the settlements themselves, it has refused to intervene when such land is taken on the grounds that it is needed in order to protect the settlements.[364] Hence large tracts of private Palestinian land have been seized as part of what may be called "the settlement project".[365] While refusing to rule on the argument that use of public land for settlements is unlawful, the Court has legitimised that use in various ways.[366] The Court has upheld planning decisions in the West Bank that were adopted to implement the settlement project,[367] and also upheld a change in the law in the West Bank that caters to the interests of settlers.[368]

Before proceeding it is important to consider the restricted formal legal implications of the Court's decisions that the legality under international law of establishing settlements for Israeli civilians in occupied territory is non-justiciable. In a major judgment on the doctrine of justiciability, Justice Aharon Barak drew a distinction between two types of non-justiciability: normative non-justiciability, namely a case in which there are no legal norms on the basis of which the court can decide the case; and institutional non-justiciability, a case in which the *court* considers that it is not the appropriate institution to decide the issue before it, and should leave it to

363 David Kretzmer, 'The "Constitutional Reform" and the Occupied Territories' (2023) 56 *Israel Law Review* 397.

364 HCJ 2717/96 *Wafa v Minister of Defence* [1996] PD 50(2) 848. This case involved seizure of private land for building a by-pass road to enable settlers and other Israelis to travel without going through Palestinian areas. The Court rejected the argument that the seizure could not be justified on security rounds and mentioned that the court had already held a number of times that it would not interfere in seizure of land for by-pass roads.

365 B'Tselem, 'Land Grab: Israel's Settlement Policy in the West Bank' (May 2002) <https://www.btselem.org/download/200205_land_grab_eng.pdf> accessed 16 January 2025; Kerem Navot and B'Tselem, 'This Is Ours - And This Too – Israel's Settlement Policy in the West Bank' (March 2021) <https://www.keremnavot.org/_files/ugd/a76eb4_1bb3fac3cb4f4363a88a34ea6ffaf7cd.pdf> accessed 16 January 2025.

366 Kretzmer and Ronen (n 57) 489.

367 ibid ch 13.

368 HCJ 358/18 *Hebron Municipality v State of Israel* [30 June 2019].

be decided by the other organs of the state.[369] It is clear from the reasoning of the Court in the leading *Bargil* case, that the Court was referring to institutional non-justiciability. Hence accepting the non-justiciability argument meant only that the *Court* should not decide the issue; not that the settlements are necessarily legal or illegal under international law, but that the question of their legality should be considered by other branches of government, first and foremost amongst which is the executive. This is not, however, the way government's legal advisers perceive the issue. The fact that the Supreme Court will not intervene in the decision to establish settlements means in their eyes that they too may ignore the question of the settlements' legality under international law. Thus, for example, the team appointed by the government to consider regulating the use of land in the West Bank claimed that while it would consider issues of customary international law, it would not question the legality of establishing settlements, since the Supreme Court had decided that the issue was non-justiciable.[370] From discussions with government lawyers and legal opinions that have been published, it is clear that the question the legal advisers ask themselves is whether the Supreme Court is likely to intervene in a given decision.[371] Once the Court held that the legality of the settlements in international

369 HCJ 910/86 *Ressler v Minister of Defence* [1988] PD 42(2) 441. Justice Barak was of the opinion that no issue can be non-justiciable on normative grounds, since there are always legal norms on which a court may decide whether a given action or decision is lawful or not. This was not accepted by all the other justices on the bench.

370 Expert Team for Consolidating a Blueprint for Regularization of Construction in Judea and Samaria (*Zandberg Report*) (15 February 2018) <https://www.gov.il/BlobFolder/reports/report_11/he/report_11.pdf> [in Hebrew] accessed 16 January 2025. The team also misrepresented the grounds on which the Court decided that the issue of settlements was non-justiciable. While the Court ruled that the grounds were that the dominant nature of the issue is political, according to the team the grounds were that the issue is subject to public controversy: ibid para 9. The Supreme Court has never decided that public controversy over an issue makes the issue non-justiciable.

371 See, eg, two letters of the Attorney General addressing questions concerning settlements. Even when referring to international law the emphasis was on whether it would be the basis for the Supreme Court to intervene in a decision of the government. See Letter of Attorney General dated 25 February 1980 (n 358) and Letter of Attorney General dated 12 May 1980 (n 299).

law is non-justiciable this question was, and continues to be, ignored by government legal advisers.[372]

In discussing the settlements it is also important to note that the implications of the Israeli settlements in the West Bank go far beyond the question of their legality under international law. There are now about 500,000 Israelis settled in the West Bank (not including East Jerusalem) who are subject to a different legal regime than the regime that applies to the local Palestinian population. Furthermore, the use of violence against Palestinians and their property by settlers has been endemic to the system since the early years of the occupation. Below we discuss the systematic failure of the authorities to enforce the law against members of the settler community who have used violence against Palestinians or their property.

7.4 The Court's Spoke in the Wheel: The Lawyers Help Out

The Court's decision in the *Elon Moreh* case that seizure of private land for the establishment of a settlement was unlawful caused a major upheaval. Various proposals were aired, including a proposal that legislation be passed to abolish the Court's jurisdiction to review actions in the occupied territory.[373] Prime Minister Begin was not prepared to take such measures. He made it clear that the Court's order to evacuate the settlement would be respected.[374] At the same time he demanded that a way should be found to continue with the settlement project without violating the principle behind the Court's judgment.

In a special meeting of the Cabinet to discuss the implications of the judgment, the Attorney General explained that the Court's decision only related to private land.[375] He opined that if the government wished to continue to establish settlements it should do so on public land. The Attorney General failed to mention that Justice Landau had stated that there was a second reason why the establishment of the settlement was unlawful, namely that no military regime may create facts in occupied territory that

372 As noted below (n 377) the letter of the Attorney General dated 12 May 1980 was written before the leading judgment of the Supreme Court in which it held that the legality of settlements is non-justiciable.

373 Letter of Attorney General (n 358).

374 See minutes of Cabinet meeting 8/5740 (1 November 1979) <https://search.archives.gov.il/search/090717068a7296b2> [in Hebrew] accessed 16 January 2025.

375 ibid.

are intended to remain after the occupation ends.[376] Nor did he mention the prohibition in international law on establishing settlements in occupied territory, and the restriction on use of public land in occupied territory.[377] To the best of my knowledge, no legal opinion was ever sought whether using public land to build houses for the citizens of the occupying power is compatible with Article 55 of the Hague Regulations.[378] The Supreme Court refused to address this question on the grounds that the Palestinian petitioner who raised it did not have standing to do so.[379]

---

376 In a legal opinion that the Attorney General wrote a few months after the Cabinet discussion he quoted the part of the judgment in which Justice Landau had referred to the "insuperable legal obstacle" created by the intention of permanence, and asked how one could establish a settlement on land that had been seized on a temporary basis. The answer he gave was the answer on temporariness that the Court gave in the *Beth El* case (n 236) that was decided before the *Elon Moreh* case (n 151), namely that the settlement could only remain as long as Israel retained control over the area. See letter of Attorney General, dated 25 February 1980 (n 358). There are two problems with this opinion. Firstly, the AG restricted the implications of Justice Landau's legal obstacle to seizure of private land, whereas Justice Landau mentioned a general principle in the law of occupation that stands in the way of use of "state land" as well. Secondly, the *Elon Moreh* decision rejected the test of temporariness adopted in the *Beth El* case, in favour of a test that rests on the intention, rather than the theoretical chance that the settlement will be removed if Israel relinquishes control over the area.

377 While in the Cabinet meeting the Attorney General did not mention the restrictions in international law on establishing settlements for civilians of the occupying power, a few months later the Prime Minister asked him whether it would be legal to expropriate private land in the West Bank in order to establish Israeli settlements. In his letter dated 12 May 1980 (n 299) the Attorney General gave a negative answer to this question, relying, inter alia, on texts on the law of occupation. The Attorney General also mentioned Article 49(1) of GCIV and stated that the Supreme Court had not decided whether this provision applies to establishment of Israeli settlements in the West Bank (his letter was written before the leading decision that held that this question is non-justiciable).

378 In HCJ 285/81 *Al-Nazer v IDF Commander in Judea and Samaria* [1982] PD 36(1) 701, Justice Shamgar referred to the issue of public land. He explained that the terms "administration" and "usufruct" mentioned in Article 55 "do indeed prohibit the sale or transfer of ownership in some other way, but that on the other hand they permit, for example, renting, leasing or working the land" (ibid 704). He did not refer to allocating the land for the use of citizens of the occupying power, or to changing the whole character of the land by building a settlement on it.

379 *Ghrayeb* case (n 274). Also see the judgment of Justice Mazza in *'Ayyad* case (n 274). This case involved a plan to build a settlement on public land in the West Bank. Justice Mazza held that since they could not prove the harm caused to their interests by the plan, Palestinian villagers could not challenge the plan on the grounds that it was incompatible with international law.

The Cabinet accepted the Attorney General's opinion that under the *Elon Moreh* precedent the only restriction on establishing settlements in the occupied territory relates to use of private land for this purpose. Determined to proceed with the settlement project, the Cabinet passed a formal resolution according to which the settlement project would be expanded "by adding people to the existing settlements and establishing new settlements on land of the state."[380]

The Court's decision in the *Elon Moreh* case seemed on its face to be a victory for legal values over political decisions that violate individual rights. However, not only did the decision not lead to restraints on the government's settlement policy; it had the opposite effect.[381] The Cabinet decision to expand the settlement project by building settlements on what was termed "state land" led to an increased effort to declare land to be "government property" and to establish settlements on such land. How was this achieved?

7.5 "State Land" Policy

Soon after the occupation began, a military order was promulgated concerning "government property."[382] According to this order a Custodian of Government Property appointed by the military commander was authorised to take possession of government property and to regulate its use. Later a provision was added to the military order that stipulated that if the

---

380 The term "state land" is not a legal term. Under a military order promulgated in the West Bank land may be recognized as "government land", which will then be administered by the Custodian of Government Property appointed by the military commander. Use of the term "state land", rather than the legal term "government property", is clearly politically motivated to create the impression that such land belongs to the State of Israel, since the government does not recognize any other state with a legitimate claim to rights in the West Bank.

381 See Shlomo Gazit, *Trapped Fools: Thirty Years of Israeli Policies in the Territories* (Routledge 1999) 246: "the HCJ ruling in the *Elon Moreh* case only promoted the government's policy. It brought an end to the process in which, for some 11 years, the government concealed its real intentions regarding settlement, under the guise of baseless security claims." The author, Shlomo Gazit, served as Co-Ordinator of Government Activities in the Territories at the time of the Elon Moreh case. Also see Shlomit-Greenfield-Gilat, 'The Flap of the butterfly's Wing in HCJ Dweikat' *Roots in the Law* (Ministry of Justice, 20 March 2019) <https://www.gov.il/he/pages/roots_1979> [in Hebrew] accessed 16 January 2025.

382 *Order Relating to Government Property (Area of West Bank) (no. 59)*,1967.

Custodian certified property to be "government property" the onus was on anyone who challenged the certification to prove otherwise. This placed a heavy burden on Palestinian land owners since only one third of the land in the West Bank had been registered when Israel occupied the area in 1967, and one of the IDF first moves was to halt the land registration process that the Jordanians had initiated.[383] Persons who wished to prove that they owned unregistered land had to produce a *koushan* (title deed) or to prove that they had possessed and worked the land for an uninterrupted period of at least ten years.

The definition of "government property" in the original military order only included land that belonged to an enemy state (in this context, Jordan) on the day the IDF took control of the West Bank in June 1967. According to data published by the Co-ordinator of Government Activities in the Territories, in 1973 there were only 678,021 dunams of government land in the West Bank, and most of this land was not suitable for cultivation.[384] In order to implement the government decision to expand settlements by building on "state land", a way had to be found to expand the definition of government property.[385] Once again the lawyers came to the rescue. They adopted two connected tactics. Firstly, the military order on government property was amended so as to include not only property that had belonged to the Jordanian government in June 1967, but land that belonged to the government after that date.[386] Secondly, the Ottoman Land Law that still applied in the West Bank in 1967 was exploited so that land that had not been cultivated continuously for a period of 10 years, or even if it had been cultivated for this period, subsequently had not been cultivated for 3 years, would be declared to be "state land".[387]

383 Kretzmer and Ronen (n 57) 206-207.

384 B'Tselem, *Under the Guise of Legality: Israel's Declarations of State Land in the West Bank* (February 2012) 13 <https://www.btselem.org/download/201203_under_the_guise_of_legality_eng.pdf> accessed 16 January 2025.

385 Gazit (n 381) 244-246.

386 *Order Relating to Government Property (Amendment no. 7) (no. 1091)*, 1984.

387 See B'Tselem (n 384); The Ottoman Land Law recognized five categories of land: *wakf, miri, mulk, mawat* and *matrouk*. Most of the land that was not in towns or cities was *miri* land. Such land in theory belonged to the Sultan but a person who cultivated the land for a period of ten years acquired what amounted to virtual ownership in the land. The policy of declaring uncultivated land to be "state land" (see n 380) related first and foremost to *miri* land. A full description of the process of declaring land to be "state land" is provided in the *Zandberg Report* (n 370), and in the Response of the Attorney General to the petition in *Silwad* case (n 304) <https://law.acri.org.il/he/wp-content/uploads/2017/11/bagatz2055-17-hoq-haha

The lawyers provided the government with the legal framework for expanding the settlement project without examining whether the actions they recommended were compatible with Israel's international obligations as an occupying power. The government exploited this legal framework in order to gain control over huge areas of land that was used for Israeli settlements.[388] While public property in occupied territory should be used for the benefit of the local population, statistics provided in 2013 by the Civil Administration that is part of the military government in the West Bank show that 99.75% of the government land that has been allocated for private use has been allocated to Israelis or Israeli settlement organizations.[389]

Declaring land to be government property was not the only tool devised by lawyers to enable the government to lay its hands on land to be used for Israeli settlements.[390] Other tools included declaring land to be absentee property that passed to the control of the Custodian of Absentee Property;[391] declaring land to be part of a nature reserve;[392] declaring large areas of land to be "firing zones";[393] expropriating land for public needs, the

---

sdara-yoamash1117.pdf> accessed 15 January 2025. Also see Neve Gordon (n 68) 128-131; Eldar and Zertal (n 245) 361-371. In an interview for the film "The Law in these Parts" a person who was a government lawyer at the time of the *Elon Moreh* case, proudly claimed that in a meeting in which Ariel Sharon, at the time the minister in charge of settlement, demanded a solution to the problem that arose after the judgment in that case, he came up with the idea of grabbing *mawat* land for settlements. The interview is available at <https://www.thelawfilm.com/inside/clip/if-it-werent-legal-the-high-court-of-justice-wouldnt-allow-it> accessed 16 January 2025. *Mawat* land ("dead land") is land that is not cultivated or owned by anyone and is one and a half km from a village. All *mawat* land is regarded as government property: Response of the Attorney General, ibid para 19.

388 According to the Settlement Watch project of Peace Now, 1,400,000 dunams of land have been declared "state land" in the West Bank: <https://peacenow.org.il/state-land-allocation> [in Hebrew] accessed 16 January 2025. This amounts to almost 25% of the land in the West Bank.

389 The data were provided to the Movement on Freedom of Information following a demand under the Freedom of Information Law: <https://www.meida.org.il/8531> [in Hebrew] accessed 16 January 2025.

390 Neve Gordon (n 68) 120.

391 Kretzmer and Ronen (n 57) 207; B'Tselem, 'Land Grab' (n 365).

392 'Land Grab' ibid.

393 See *Abu Aram* case (n 98) and the discussion of this case by Ben-Naftali and Diamond (n 98). The connection between declaring land to be a "firing zone" and the settlement policy was made clear in a meeting of the Ministerial Committee on Settlement in 1979, in which Ariel Sharon declared: "As the person who initiated the military fire zones in 1967, they were all intended for one purpose: to provide an opportunity for Jewish settlement in the area." <https://www.972mag.com/firing-z

public need being construction of a highway that facilitates access to a settlement;[394] and allowing and facilitating purchase of private land by Israeli citizens.[395] When used together, all these methods enabled the Israeli authorities to gain possession of large tracts of land in the West Bank that is used solely for settlements and other projects serving Israeli interests, or in which residential use by Palestinians is barred.[396]

7.6 Unauthorised Outposts

According to a 1996 decision of the Cabinet, no new settlements were to be established in the West Bank, and no existing settlements to be expanded, without the approval of the Cabinet, or the Minister of Defence.[397] Until

---

ones-sharon-settlements/> accessed 16 January 2025. Also see minutes of a later meeting in which Sharon stated that he told the IDF representative that an area in the South Hebron hills should be declared as a firing zone, so that the Palestinians could be evacuated from the area: <https://www.akevot.org.il/news-item/document-revealed-by-akevot-ariel-sharon-instructed-idf-to-create-training-zone-to-displace-palestinians/> [in Hebrew]; <https://www.972mag.com/explainer-masafer-yatta-firing-zone-918/> accessed 16 January 2025.

394 See *Tabeeb* case (n 308).

395 Gazit (n 381) 244-245; B'Tselem, 'Land Grab' (n 365) 62-3. A military order issued in 1967 prohibited land transactions in the West Bank without the written authorization of the military commander: *Order Regarding Land Transactions (Judea and Samaria) (No. 25)*, 1967. Authorization to purchase private land was only granted to a company owned by the Jewish National Fund (JNF). This policy was changed in the early nineteen-eighties after the Ministerial Committee on Settlement decided to encourage establishment of settlements in the West Bank as a private enterprise. B'tselem, 'Land Grab', ibid.

396 By 2018, 1,400,000 dunams had been declared "state lands" (i.e. government property) (n 388) and in 2024 another 23,700 dunams were declared "state land": <https://peacenow.org.il/en/state-land-declaration-12000-dunams> accessed 16 January 2025. This means that approximately 34% of the land in the West Bank, amounting to approximately 50% of the land in Area C, have been declared "state land." By 2022, 383,600 dunams had been declared to be nature reserves: <https://peacenow.org.il/en/the-minister-of-defense-approved-the-declaration-of-the-largest-nature-reserve-in-25-years-in-the-west-bank> accessed 16 January 2025; roughly 18% of the lands in the West Bank have been declared to be "firing zones": <https://jstreet.org/israeli-firing-zones-and-displacement-of-palestinians-in-the-west-bank/> accessed 16 January 2025.

397 Talia Sasson, 'Interim Report on Unauthorized Outposts' (8 March 2005) (*Sasson Report*) in Hebrew]. English summary is available at <http://www.mfa.gov.il/mfa/aboutisrael/state/law/pages/summary%20of%20opinion%20concerning%20unauthorized%20outposts%20-%20talya%20sason%20adv.aspx>. For the various

1992 this policy was largely respected, but after the Rabin government that came to power in that year placed a freeze on new settlements in the West Bank, nationalistic groups began to establish "outposts" in the area.[398] Although these outposts did not receive the formal approval required under the Cabinet decision, they could not have been established without the tacit or explicit consent of the Civil Administration. Hence, it is clear that in most, if not all, cases, the settlers enjoyed such consent. They also received financial and other measures of support from government departments, Ministry of Defence officials, the Settlement Division of the World Zionist Organization (WZO), the Jewish National Fund (JNF), the regional councils of Israeli West Bank settlements and settler movements.[399]

Ariel Sharon had been one of the main supporters of settlements in general, and of grabbing land and establishing outposts on it.[400] After he became prime minister in 2001, the Bush administration pressured him to evacuate the unauthorized outposts, which, in the mind of the US administration, were an obstacle to the two-state solution favoured by the international community. In a somewhat cynical move Sharon requested

---

Cabinet resolutions on authorisation for establishment or extension of settlements see 'Report on the Status of Building in the Area of Judea and Samaria' (*Levy Report*) (n 157).

398 According to an NGO report, the establishment of unauthorised outposts intensified after Benjamin Netanyahu became prime minister in 1996. His government decided to resume building settlements, but only those authorised by the Cabinet. Peace Now, 'Return of the Outpost Method' (July 2019) <http://peacenow.org.il/wp-content/uploads/2019/08/maahazim-english_full.pdf> accessed 16 January 2025. On the background to the proliferation of unauthorised outposts and the military authorities' response to the phenomenon, including the conflict they encountered with the political echelons, see Ronit Levine-Schnur, 'Private Property and Public Power in the Occupied West Bank' (2017) 6 *European Property Law Journal* 122; Peace Now, Unravelling the Mechanism behind Illegal Outposts (2017) <https://peacenow.org.il/wp-content/uploads/2017/03/unraveling-the-mechanism-behind-illegal-outpots-full-report-1.pdf> accessed 16 January 2025.

399 *Sasson Report* (n 397); Erez Tzfadia, 'The Gray Space of the Settlement in the Territories: A Geographic-Legal Analysis of the Outposts" (2016) 47 *Theory and Crticism* 133; Hilo Glazer and Hagar Shizaf, 'The Netanyahu Government does not merely enable Jewish terror in the West Bank: It finances it' *Ha'aretz Supplement* (10 October 2024) <https://www.haaretz.co.il/magazine/2024-10-10/ty-article-magazine/.highlight/00000192-70ab-d292-a392-78bfa8210000> [in Hebrew] accessed 16 January 2025.

400 Sharon had encouraged settlers "to seize every hill in the West Bank and settle in it." His government had also financed outposts: 'Ex-minister: Sharon encouraged settlers' *TribLive* (10 March 2005) <https://archive.triblive.com/news/ex-minister-sharon-encouraged-settlers/> accessed 16 January 2025.

Talia Sasson, a former senior Ministry of Justice lawyer, to write a report on the issue.[401] Sasson located 105 unauthorised outposts in the West Bank, but wrote that she was not sure that no more such outposts existed. The outposts had not been established in compliance with the land planning laws; many were established on public land or land that had been declared "government property," but others were established on private land of Palestinians. Sasson wrote that there was no way to validate the construction of outposts that were built on private land, and that such settlements should therefore be evacuated, "the sooner the better".[402]

Despite the commitment to the US administration and the conclusions of the Sasson Report, very few outposts, and none of the larger ones, were evacuated.[403] In 2011 the government informed the Supreme Court that it had decided that all outposts on private land would be evacuated, but that it would consider retroactive approval and planning procedures for outposts built on public land or government property.[404]

In a report published in July 2019, the Settlement Watch project of the Peace Now movement reported that 32 new outposts had been established, 15 outposts had been regularized and 35 others were in the process of regularization.[405] In 2013 the Cabinet decided to establish a new settlement in the location of three unauthorised outposts. In other cases, the outpost

401 The government also directed the IDF commander in the West Bank to issue military orders which would enable him to evacuate unauthorized outposts without going through the procedure laid down in local planning laws. These military orders were challenged by Israeli settlers but were upheld by the Supreme Court: HCJ 548/04 *Amana, The Settlement Movement of Gush Emunim v IDF Commander in Judea and Samaria* [2004] PD 58(3) 373.

402 *Sasson Report* (n 397) para 5.3. Sasson was following the prevailing view mentioned above that private land of Palestinians may not be expropriated for settlements.

403 B'Tselem, 'By Hook or by Crook' (n 346) 17. As we shall see, at a later stage, legal action was taken by Palestinian land-owners on whose land outposts had been constructed. Following court orders a few outposts were evacuated.

404 Complementary State Response to HCJ 7891/07 *Peace Now v Minister of Defence* <http://peacenow.org.il/wp-content/uploads/2011/03/StateResponse_outposts_on_private_land_will_be_evacuated070311.pdf>, para 4 [in Hebrew] accessed 16 January 2025; See also HCJ 9060/08 *Abdallah v Minister of Defence* [2012] PD 65(2) 669, paras 2-3; HCJ 9949/08 *Hammad v Minister of Defence* [25 December 2014] para 14; HCJ 5023/08 *Shehadeh v Minister of Defence* [8 February 2015] para 12.

405 Peace Now, 'Return of the Outpost Method' (n 398). "Regularization" involves approval under land planning laws, including issuing retroactive building permits for the buildings.

was validated as a neighbourhood inside an existing settlement.[406] Even after the Hamas attack of October 7 and the subsequent war in Gaza, the government continued to encourage and support the unauthorized outposts. The Cabinet decided to allocate 75 million shekels for what were termed "young settlements" (a term used to whitewash unauthorised outposts).[407] According to a recent investigative report published in *Ha'aretz*, there are now 60 so-called "shepherd's farms" in the West Bank. These "farms", which were established without planning permission, have gained effective control over vast tracts of land and have received massive funding from government ministries and the JNF.[408]

As political pressure from settlers and their supporters grew to find a way to "regularize" the unauthorised outposts, including those built on private land, in 2012 the government established the Edmond Levy committee,[409] to find a way to "legalize" unauthorized outposts.[410] The members of the

406 The three new settlements were Bruchin, Rechalim, and Sansana: Yesh Din, 'The secret life of settlement outposts' (1 April 2015) <www.yesh-din.org/en/the-secret-life-of-settlement-outposts/> accessed 16 January 2025.

407 Avi Bar-Gil, 'Another underhand move: The ministers approved transferring 75 million shekels to illegal outposts' *The Marker* (24 December 2023) <https://www.themarker.com/news/2023-12-24/ty-article/0000018c-9bb3-d9e3-a5be-fff394eb0000> [in Hebrew] accessed 16 January 2025.

408 Glazer and Shizaf (n 399); Peace Now and Kerem Navot, *The Bad Samaritan: Land Grabbing by Israeli Settlers in the Occupied West Bank Through Grazing* (December 2024) < https://peacenow.org.il/en/the-bad-samaritan-land-grabbing-by-settlers-through-grazing> accessed 15 April 2025.

409 Justice Levy was the only judge on a bench of 11 judges who had dissented in the case relating to the legality of the disengagement from Gaza, see *Gaza Coast* case (n 136). Before becoming a judge in the lower courts he had been the deputy mayor of a town on behalf of the Likud party. The other members of the Committee were the former legal adviser of the Ministry of Foreign Affairs who had written an article arguing that the settlements are legal, and a retired district court judge. According to a press report, in a Likud party meeting the Vice Prime Minister, Silvan Shalom, told the audience that the members of the Committee were hand-picked to produce the desired result: Philip Podolsky and TOI staff, 'Levy Committee that says settlements are illegal was 'rigged" *The Times of Israel* (11 December 2012) <https://www.timesofisrael.com/levy-committee-that-approved-outposts-was-rigged/> accessed 13 January 2025.

410 *Levy Report* (n 157). The political pressure included a letter to the prime minister signed by 38 cabinet ministers and Knesset members urging the prime minister to ensure that "there would be no more demolitions in Judea and Samaria". Pinhas Wolf, 'Netanyahu surrenders to pressure: he is examining legitimising West Bank outposts' *Walla News* (11 October 2011) <https://news.walla.co.il/item/1867554> [in Hebrew] accessed 16 January 2025.

Committee were obviously aware that under the law of belligerent occupation there was no way that private land of Palestinians could be expropriated for settlement purposes. They therefore took a radical line, and on the basis of flimsy arguments, and without taking account of the numerous Supreme Court judgments on the issue, previous legal opinions of the Attorney General, and the views of the ICJ and the UN Security Council, they opined that the West Bank is not occupied territory. They concluded that there were no legal impediments to building Israeli settlements in the West Bank, and that when settlements had been established on private Palestinian land, in "appropriate cases" the authorities should consider expropriating the land and paying compensation to the Palestinian land-owners.[411]

The Levy Report was heavily criticized.[412] Even the pro-settlement government of Prime Minister Netanyahu was hesitant formally to adopt the Report. Although in practice steps were taken to implement some of its proposals,[413] the government's legal advisers were of the opinion that the outposts established on private land could not be legitimized, since the consistent view of the government's legal advisers had always been that it is illegal to expropriate private land for establishment of new settlements.[414]

When Palestinian land-owners and Israeli NGOs petitioned the Supreme Court demanding that the authorities take steps to evacuate buildings

411 *Levy Report* (n 157) para 58.

412 eg, Juan Pedro Schaerer, 'The Levy Report vs. International Law' Ha'aretz (4 November 2012) <https://www.haaretz.com/opinion/juan-pedro-schaerer-the-occupation-exists-1.5196129> accessed 16 January 2025 (at the time the writer was the head of the ICRC delegation to Israel and the Occupied Territories); Yaël Ronen, 'The Levy Report: A Broken Reed' (The Forum for Regional Thinking 2012); Ben-Naftali and Reznik (n 157); Yesh Din, Unprecedented (n 157).

413 Yesh Din, 'From Occupation to Annexation: the silent adoption of the Levy Report on retroactive authorization of illegal construction in the West Bank' (2 February 2016) <https://s3-eu-west-1.amazonaws.com/files.yesh-din.org/%D7%9E%D7%9B%D7%99%D7%91%D7%95%D7%A9+%D7%9C%D7%A1%D7%99%D7%A4%D7%95%D7%97/From+Occupation+to+Annexation+English+Yesh+Din.pdf> accessed 16 January 2025.

414 This view was presented in the Letter of the Attorney General dated 12 May 1980 (n 299). In his letter the Attorney General cited the work of Gerhard von Glahn, *The Occupation of Enemy Property* (University of Minnesota Press 1957) and the US Army Manual (1956). As the Attorney General explained, an occupying power may only expropriate land if it is in accordance with the local law in the occupied territory and is done in the interests of the local population. See Dinstein (n 1) 225 (who refers to the "public interest"); *Silwad* case (n 304) paras 68-70 in opinion of Chief Justice Hayut.

constructed on private land,[415] the Attorney General was adamant that the government had no valid defence against such petitions. Hence the authorities conceded that they would evacuate unauthorised outposts built on private land. In most of these cases the government stipulated a date by which the outpost would be evacuated and the Court delivered a judgment ordering evacuation by that date. In a few cases, after the Court had granted multiple applications for extension of the date in the Court orders, the Court refused to grant further extensions and ordered the authorities to evacuate the unauthorized outpost and return the land to its Palestinian owners.[416]

In all the cases in which the Court ordered evacuation of outposts, it did so after the government had admitted that the outpost must be evacuated, but had dragged its feet in carrying out the evacuation. Nevertheless, evacuation of unauthorized outposts under court order created tremendous antagonism in right-wing and settler circles, both towards the Court and towards the Attorney General's office which represents the authorities in court. Since the Levy Report had largely been discredited, the government appointed a task force of lawyers whose mandate was to seek ways to legalize buildings and neighbourhoods that had been constructed without formal government approval and planning permission.[417] In a more drastic move, in 2017 the *Knesset* enacted legislation that obliged the military commander to expropriate private land on which unauthorized outposts had been established and to give approval to outposts established on public land.[418] Enactment of a law by the *Knesset* that violates the rights of Palestinians in the West Bank, and that flies in the face of the international law of belligerent occupation, was unprecedented. The Attorney General, who represents the government in all litigation, informed the government that he could not and would not defend it from challenges against the law in Court.

415 HCJ 7891/07 *Peace Now v Minister of Defence* (partial judgment, 18 November 2013); HCJ 8887/06 *Al-Nabot v Minister of Defence* [2 August 2011]; *Abdallah* case (n 404); *Hammad* case (n 404).

416 eg HCJ 7891/07 *Peace Now v Minister of Defence* (final judgment, 7 July 2014); *Abdallah* case (n 404); *Hammad* case (n 404); *Al-Nabot* case (n 415).

417 For the report of this team see *Zandberg Report* (n 370).

418 *Law Regulating Settlement in Judea and Samaria*, 2017. The law also obliges the authorities to declare land on which an outpost had been built as government land if there is no registered owner in the land or persons who can prove that they were entitled to registration of the land in their names. Land expropriated under the law, or declared as government land, must then be allocated for the use of the settlers.

A number of petitions were submitted to the Supreme Court challenging the validity of the law. The government was represented in court by a private lawyer, while the Attorney General's representative argued that the legislation was unconstitutional in that it violated the rights to property and equality protected in the Basic Law: Human Dignity and Liberty, and did not meet the demands of the limitations clause in that Basic Law.[419] One of the Attorney General's arguments was that the legislation did not meet the demand of proportionality, since in many cases a defence based on the concrete facts could prevent evacuation of the outpost. Hence there were less drastic means of protecting settlers who had established homes on private land than a general law that would involve expropriation of all private land on which settlers had built homes.[420]

In a majority decision of eight of the nine judges on the bench, the Court accepted the Attorney General's argument that the legislation was incompatible with the Basic Law: Human Dignity and Liberty, since it violated the rights to property and to equality of the Palestinian land-owners and failed to meet the demands of the limitations clause.[421] Having decided that the legislation was invalid on these grounds, the Court refrained from considering an argument raised by petitioners, and in an *amicus curiae* brief submitted by law professors. The argument was that the Knesset lacks the authority to pass legislation that violates the rights of the population in occupied territory, and that in all events all legislation relating to the occupied territory, whether by military order or by the legislature of the occupying power, must meet the demands of the international law of belligerent occupation.

During the years 2015-2019, when the law on "regularization" of outposts was enacted and declared invalid by the Supreme Court, the Minister of Justice was Ayelet Shaked. Shaked was determined to further the government settlement policy and to find a legal solution for what she called

419 According to section 8 of *Basic Law: Human Dignity and Liberty,* a limitation on a protected right is not valid unless it is prescribed by a law, enacted for a proper purpose and meets the demands of proportionality. The Attorney General also rested part of his argument on the strong protection of property in occupied territory under the law of belligerent occupation: Response of Attorney General in *Silwad* case (n 387) paras 113-121.

420 Under the jurisprudence of the Supreme Court the proportionality of a restriction on a protected right is assessed by the three-prong test adopted in German and Canadian law. A measure will not be regarded as proportionate if the legitimate purpose of the law could be achieved by less drastic means.

421 *Silwad* case (n 304) paras 149-155 in opinion of Chief Justice Hayut.

the "young settlements". She demanded that lawyers in the Attorney General's office find a way to defend government policy before the Court.[422] Once again, lawyers came to the rescue. They now raised an argument for defending outposts built on private Palestinian land that relied on a military order that was meant to protect the Custodian of Government Property who had allocated land in good faith if it transpired that the land was not government property.[423] The argument that was raised now was that if settlers had settled in good faith on private land allocated to them by the Custodian, they would be protected against a claim by the land owners to evict them. Having been provided with the defence by lawyers in the Ministry of Justice, in one case the government changed course during the court proceedings. While it had originally conceded that housing in a settlement that had been built on private Palestinian land should be evacuated, government lawyers now raised the "good faith" argument. The argument was accepted by the district court.[424] On appeal the Supreme Court rejected the argument,[425] but in a further hearing before an expanded bench the majority in the Court upheld it.[426] This is as clear a case as could be of how the lawyers joined together not only to support the settlement project, but to grant protection to Israeli settlers who had taken over Palestinian land. As Ronit Levine-Shnur argues, the argument raised by the Attorney General, and accepted eventually by the Supreme Court, according to which a military order can grant protection to civilians of the occupying power who take over land belonging to local inhabitants in the occupied territory, flies in the face of customary international law that obliges the occupying power to respect private property and not to change the local law in occupied territory unless it is absolutely prevented

422 See Ayelet Shaked, 'HCJ Ofra Case is just the beginning' *Makor Rishon* (9 January 2020) <https://www.makorrishon.co.il/opinion/196051/> [in Hebrew] accessed 16 January 2025.

423 Ronit Levine-Schnur, 'On 'Market Overt' in Land in Judea and Samaria' (2020) 50 *Mishpatim* 307 [in Hebrew].

424 HCJ 419/14 *Silwad Municipality v Minister of Defence* [6 January 2020]. According to Shaked (n 422) this change was a result of her demands for legal backing of the government's settlement policy. For an incisive and devastating criticism of the court's judgment in this case see Ronit Levine-Schnur, 'On the District Court Decision in the Matter of Mitzpe Kramim' (2018) 86 *Human Rights Case Reviews* 4 <https://zola.colman.ac.il/wp-content/uploads/2018/12/86_3levin.pdf> [in Hebrew] accessed 16 January 2025.

425 HCJ 953/11, CA 766/18 *Salkha v Minister of Defence* [27 August 2020].

426 FHCA 6364/20 *Minister of Defence v Salkha* [27 July 2022].

from doing so.[427] As mentioned above, in supporting his argument that the Regularization Law was invalid, the Attorney General argued that there were less drastic means of protecting settlers who were living in houses built on private land of Palestinians. One of the means he mentioned was the "good faith" argument.[428]

To summarize: despite the original government decision that all settlements in the West Bank must receive prior approval by the Cabinet or the Minister of Defence, well over a hundred outposts have been established without such formal approval. The attitude of the government in supporting these outposts, and later deciding to regularize them, lends credence to the view that establishing such outposts is in effect a part of the government's policy in the West Bank.[429] The government's lawyers have worked to provide legal backing for this policy, despite the fact that the policy flies in the face of international law and that giving retroactive approval to illegal acts is a blow to the rule of law. The Supreme Court did indeed frustrate the attempt to give blanket approval to the outposts by legislation, and ordered evacuation of outposts when the government conceded that they were built on private Palestinian land. However, it lent its hand to retroactive approval

---

427 Levine-Schnur (n 423). Also see the *amicus curiae* brief to the Court in the appeal in *Salkha* case (n 425) submitted by Yesh Din and the Association for Civil Rights in Israel, <https://www.nevo.co.il/psika_html/kitvey/kt-18-7668-11.pdf> [in Hebrew] accessed 16 January 2025. Aware of the limits on the power of the military commander in occupied territory to change the local law, and of his duty to protect private property, the judges in the Supreme Court who rejected the good faith argument claimed that the provision on good faith in the military order must be given a strict interpretation. See the judgments of Chief Justice Hayut in *Salkha* case (n 425) and of Deputy Chief Justice Vogelman in FHCA *Salkha* (n 426). They refrained from ruling that under the local land law in the West Bank, the good faith argument is not a defence when a person has built on *miri* land that does not belong to him/her (as explained in the Response of Attorney General (n 387) para 45), and that therefore the military order on good faith is incompatible with the duty of the occupying power not to change the local law unless absolutely prevented from doing so.

428 Response of Attorney General in *Silwad* case (n 387) paras 150-155. The AG's argument was that the legislation that violated various rights of the Palestinians did not meet the demands of the limitations clause in the *Basic Law: Human Dignity and Liberty*. The reason was that the law was not the least harmful way of protecting the Israeli settlers from evacuation from unauthorised settlements, since ostensibly the good faith provision in the military order "could provide a significant solution to a large proportion of the cases in which the Custodian [of Government Property] and the settler acted in good faith, and it transpired later that the land was not government property." (ibid para 151).

429 See Erez Tzfadia (n 399); Glazer and Shizaf (399).

of outposts by accepting the "good faith" argument and refusing to consider petitions demanding evacuation of all unauthorized settlements. It has also refused to order the authorities to evacuate unauthorized outposts built on government property, and has conceded that an outpost on such land should not be evacuated if the government intends to "regularize" it.[430] The ineluctable conclusion is that both government lawyers and the Supreme Court have played a central role in legitimizing the settlement project of successive Israeli governments.

7.7 Settler Violence

The establishment of settlements for citizens of the occupying power in the occupied West Bank has created a situation in which two groups live side by side: the local population who perceive the military rulers as part of a "hostile army," and who have no political rights in Israel, and the Israeli settlers, who have such rights, and view the military as "their army." This inherent imbalance has deepened since the introduction of a number of mechanisms aimed at applying Israeli law to the settlers and the settlements.[431] The Supreme Court recognized that different legal regimes apply to Israeli settlers and the local Palestinian population, but did not seem to find it problematic.[432] The existence in the same territory of two populations, distinguished on ethnic/national grounds but subject to different legal regimes, provides the basis for the claim that the regime in the West Bank constitutes apartheid.[433] Even if one rejects such an assertion, a UN independent fact-finding mission showed that the Israeli settlements in the

430 *Peace Now* case, final judgment (n 416); Kretzmer and Ronen (n 57) 290-294.

431 Benvenisti (n 1) 233–235; Association for Civil Rights in Israel, 'One Rule, Two Legal Systems: Israel's Regime of Laws in the West Bank' (October 2014) <https://law.acri.org.il/en/wp-content/uploads/2015/02/Two-Systems-of-Law-English-FINAL.pdf> accessed 16 January 2025.

432 *Hebron Municipality* case (n 368).

433 See eg John Dugard and John Reynolds, 'Apartheid, Internationial Law, and the Occupied Palestinian Territory' (2013) 24 *European Journal of International Law* 867; Oren Yiftachel, 'Creeping Apartheid? Regime, Space and Citizenship in Israel/Palestine' (2018) 13 *Public Space* 139; Michael Sfard, 'The Israeli Occupation of the West Bank and the Crime of Apartheid: Legal Opinion' (Yesh Din June 2020) <https://s3-eu-west-1.amazonaws.com/files.yesh-din.org/Apartheid+2020/Apartheid+ENG.pdf> accessed 16 January 2025. The ICJ was not prepared to say that Israel had instituted apartheid in the West Bank, but thought it sufficient to state that it was violating Article 3 of the International Convention for the Elimination of all Forms

West Bank have had a disastrous effect on the rights and liberties of the Palestinian inhabitants.[434]

The international law of belligerent occupation relies on a balance between the military needs of the occupying power and the benefit of the local population. It places serious limitations on the scope of governmental authority of the occupying power. When the relevant restrictions are ignored, this body of norms may be used solely as an instrument that legitimizes limitations on the rights of local population in the occupied territory.[435] It thus becomes clear why when defending its actions in the West Bank before the Supreme Court, the government continues to rely on a pretence of adherence to the law of belligerent occupation. Occupation law is used to exploit the power of an occupant to seize land ostensibly for military purposes, to place heavy restrictions on the rights and liberties of the local population, and to justify long-term rule over Palestinians in the West Bank without their enjoyment of political rights in the state that controls their lives.[436]

The military authorities' failure to protect West Bank Palestinians from the violence of Israeli settlers reached the Supreme Court and Israeli civil authorities in the early eighties of the last century, when a case concerning a building in the centre of Hebron, the largest city in the West Bank, first reached the Supreme Court. The Hadassah building belonged to Jews before the 1948 war. Following the 1949 Armistice Agreement, when Jordan ruled the West Bank, the Hadassah building was administered by the Jordanian Custodian of Enemy Property. The Custodian leased the building to an organization that rented out the shops in the building to local merchants. After the Likud came to power in 1977 pressure was placed on the government to allow Jews to settle in the centre of Hebron, especially in the Hadassah building. Without formal government approval, a group of Jewish women entered the top floor of the building and refused to leave it. The government gave in to political pressure and decided to add a floor to the building and to establish a *yeshiva* (religious academy) in the building.

---

of Racial Discrimination, that refers both to racial segregation and to apartheid. See Advisory Opinion, *Occupied Palestinian Territory* (n 9), paras 223-229.

434 UN Human Rights Council, 'Report of the independent international factfinding mission to investigate the implications of the Israeli settlements" (n 346).

435 David Kretzmer, 'The Law of Belligerent Occupation as a System of Control: Dressing Up Exploitation in Respectable Garb' in Daniel Bar-Tal & Izhak Schnell (eds), *The Impacts of Lasting Occupation: Lessons from Israeli Society* (OUP 2013) 31.

436 ibid.

Senior legal advisers warned that steps should be taken to ensure that settling of Jews in the building would not harm the merchants who had stores on the ground floor.[437]

In 1981 a number of Hebron residents, including owners of stores in the Hadassah building, petitioned the Supreme Court to order evacuation of the settlers from the building. They provided evidence, which, according to the Court, seemed weighty, that the settlers were harassing the Palestinians who occupied part of the building. Thus, for example, store-owners showed that the settlers on the top floor had caused damage to the ceiling of their store and that merchandise had disappeared from the store. One store owner complained to the authorities that settlers had pushed him and demanded that he hand his store to them. The Court mentioned that the merchant's complaint has not been adequately addressed. After government counsel gave an undertaking that steps would be taken to protect the Palestinian tenants and that their complaints would be investigated, the Court decided to accept this undertaking, and not to issue a court order in the matter. Nevertheless the Court saw fit to remark:

> There is no doubt that the main task of the sovereign in occupied territory is to protect law and order. He must do so even if no complaint had been lodged by local inhabitants. At the same time it is important to make clear to the local inhabitants that it is their right and duty to submit a complaint when they are harassed, to demand that the complaint be investigated and that action be taken on the basis of the conclusions of the investigation.
>
> Only after the learned counsel of the respondents declared before us that the investigation of the complaint about the store was re-opened, and that orders were given to take breaches of law and order seriously, we decided that there was no need to issue an order nisi in the matter. We want to believe that from now on there will be effective action, and

437 HCJ 72/86 *Zalloum v Military Commander in Judea and Samaria* [1987] PD 41(1) 528, para 3. Before allowing Israelis to settle in the building the Attorney General requested a legal opinion on the status of this building and a few other buildings in the West Bank that had belonged to Jews until 1948. In an opinion dated 8 February 1980 the Deputy Attorney General wrote that part of the building had been leased to UNWRA. No mention was made of the stores on the ground floor mentioned by the parties in court. The opinion is available at <https://search.archives.gov.il/search/0b071706808b9f90> [in Hebrew] accessed 16 January 2025, 165.

> that the offenders will be prosecuted. This is the only way to ensure that things will calm down and order will be restored.[438]

The apparent assumption of the Court was that the authorities would indeed change their conduct and that the harassment would end without forcing evacuation of the settlers from the building. From another case relating to the same building some years later it was clear that this assumption was false.[439] Nevertheless, when in that case the military commander declared that security measures were needed to protect the settlers in the building, the Court refused to interfere with the commander's decision, despite the serious restrictions it imposed on access to the Palestinian merchants' stores.[440]

Following its commitment to the Court in the first Hadassah case, a task force was established to monitor the handling of information on settler violence in the West Bank. This task force did not receive information on all the cases of violence against the Palestinians. Hence, according to the Karp report that we discuss below, a year after the Court's judgment, soldiers in the reserves who had served in the West Bank submitted harrowing complaints to the IDF MAG on events that were unknown to the task force.

At this time a group of Israeli law professors sent a letter to the Prime Minister and Attorney General in which they warned about settler violence towards Palestinians, and mentioned a number of concrete incidents that had not been investigated.[441] In response the Attorney General, Professor Yitzchak Zamir, appointed a monitoring team, headed by his deputy, Yehu-

---

438 HCJ 175/81 *Al Natashe v Minister of Defence* [1981] PD 35(3) 361, 363.

439 *Zalloum* case (n 437).

440 ibid. There is no doubt that in practice the security measures made the merchants' stores inaccessible to local Palestinian residents. The minister of defence had admitted in the Knesset that when the government decided to allow Jews to occupy the building a senior lawyer in the ministry of justice had warned that if they were needed, security measures should not be a nuisance to store owners. The minister stated that he was forced to prefer the advice of the military who were in charge of security even though he realised that it was incompatible with the lawyer's warning. The complicity of the Court with violence of settlers that led to the violation of the Palestinians' rights was compounded by the Court's decision to impose costs on the Palestinian petitioners. Not only should they have accepted the ruin of their businesses; they should have refrained from challenging the measures that led to their ruin in court.

441 Full disclosure: the present writer was one of the two professors who initiated sending the letter.

dit Karp, and instructed the team to write a report on law enforcement in the West Bank. The result was the Karp Report (23.5.1982).[442]

The Karp Report paints a sorry picture of acts of violence against the Palestinians that were never investigated. The report pointed to various reasons for the lack of investigations. First, despite the law that requires an investigation if the police have evidence that a felony has been committed, no investigation was carried out unless a complaint was lodged. Secondly, the military government had interfered in investigations, and there were serious flaws in many of the investigations. In addition, settlers refused to co-operate with the police, and the authorities made no attempt to arrest and question settlers who failed to respond to a demand that they appear at a police station. Lastly, investigations were drawn out, which often prevented any possibility of reaching the truth.

Most telling is the section in the Report that describes what happened in Hebron following the murder there of six Jewish *yeshiva* students. Here is what the Karp team wrote:

> We will not be fulfilling our duty to describe the nature of the acts if we do not relate to the events that occurred during the curfew in Hebron in May 1980 after the murder of the six settlers. It is indeed true that the background was traumatic, and for this reason we do not intend to present them as common events, certainly not when it comes to their scope, but they are presented here as typical of the failure to prevent brutal acts against the Arab residents and to investigate complaints in this sphere. This is especially the case since the acts were committed during a curfew. After the curfew, which lasted a few days, was lifted, local residents complained to the Hebron police on theft, robbery, causing damage to property, assaults, throwing stones and arson, which occurred during the curfew. A report dated 22.8.80 by ... a member of the IDF MAG's office, lists 13 such complaints.[443]

One might have expected, that after such a damning report, and the remarks of the Supreme Court in the case mentioned above, the authorities would make a serious effort to amend the situation, so that they could fulfil their legal obligation to protect the local population. However, about ten years after the Karp Report was presented to the Attorney General, another

442 The Report is available at <https://www.keremnavot.org/_files/ugd/cdb1a7_3342db25459b43ff8dab68d9ee20e32e.pdf> [in Hebrew] accessed 16 January 2025.

443 ibid 24.

official report described the situation in terms not that different from those of the Karp Report. This report was the report of the official Commission of Inquiry established in 1994 after a settler had entered the Cave of the Patriarchs and massacred 29 Muslims who were praying there. The Commission, which was headed by Chief Justice Meir Shamgar, president of the Supreme Court, included a section in its report on the background to the massacre in which it related to lack of law enforcement against settlers who used violence against Palestinians or their property.[444] In a Supreme Court judgement, the Court described the Shamgar report in the following manner:

> The Shamgar Report includes a wide-scale reference to the problem of law enforcement against the Israeli settlers in the area, and the Commission heard concrete claims about harassment of Palestinians by Israeli residents by physical assaults, destruction of property and uprooting of orchards. The Report also provides details on the failure to conduct police investigations, delays in investigations, failure to prosecute and more.[445]

Once again the harsh criticism of the failure of the authorities to enforce the law against settlers had no real influence on the authorities. As the Court stated:

> However, despite the frequent references in the [Shamgar] Report and on other occasions to the problems connected with law enforcement in the area, and despite steps taken in the past, the petition [in the case before the Court] reveals total failure of the respondents to enforce the law against those who breach it and cause harm to the Palestinian farmers and their property. Due to the serious violence of Israeli settlers, the personal security of the Palestinian farmers is subject to a real danger when they go out to work their land. The Palestinian farmers' property is regarded as ownerless, when after a day's work, under the cover of darkness the offenders return to the agricultural land in order to uproot trees and cause damage to agricultural tools.[446]

444 Commission of Inquiry, *Report in the Matter of the Massacre in the Cave of the Patriarchs in Hebron* (Jerusalem 1994) ch 5.

445 HCJ 9593/04 *Murar v IDF Commander in Judea and Samaria* [2006] PD 61(1) 844, para 30. English translation printed in *Oxford Reports in International Law* available at <https://opil.ouplaw.com/display/10.1093/law:ildc/452il06.case.1/law-ildc-452il06?rskey=U9LSQf&result=1&prd=ORIL> accessed January 2025.

446 ibid.

A military order promulgated by the military commander in 1967 had given law enforcement powers in the West Bank to the Israel Police. Following the Shamgar Commission of Inquiry, a new regional Israel Police command was established in the hope that it would improve enforcement of the law against the Israeli settlers. It did not do so. Many years later the State Comptroller examined the situation in the West Bank and found there was no co-ordination between the various law enforcement authorities.[447]

The mindset of the military was starkly illustrated in another case before the Supreme Court in which Palestinians once again complained that the authorities were not protecting them from settler violence and were also preventing access to their agricultural lands. Israeli settlements had been established near Palestinian villages and the military commander had placed restrictions on movement in what he deemed were "friction areas". The military commander claimed that he had to limit access to areas close to the Israeli settlements due to fear that "hostile elements" would enter them under the guise of agricultural work and attack the settlers. The commander had also imposed restrictions on the movement of Palestinians the object of which was to protect *them* from settler violence. This was too much for the Court to countenance. While it recognized the duty of the commander to protect the lives of all inhabitants of the area involved, it found that the measure used by the commander was irrational and failed to meet the proportionality test that the Supreme Court applies to measures restricting individual freedoms.[448]

Ensuring public order by a hostile army in occupied territory is complicated enough, even if there are no citizens of its own nationality living in it. The military are supposed to apply a law enforcement legal framework in carrying out this duty, not a natural role for soldiers untrained in policing methods.[449] The position of the military becomes even more complicated when it is called upon to enforce the law against its fellow citizens. In a democratic state the army is not involved in internal policing. From early on in the occupation Israeli settlers objected to the use of soldiers in remov-

447 Israeli State Comptroller's Office, 'Report no. 63b' (State Comptroller 2012) ch 3.

448 *Murar* case (n 445) paras 23-25.

449 On the legal framework for ensuring order in occupied territory see Marco Longobardo, *The Use of Armed Force in Occupied Territory* (CUP 2018); Ken Watkin, 'Maintaining Law and Order During Occupation: Breaking the Normative Chains' (2008) 41 *Israel Law Review* 175.

ing them from unauthorised settlements.[450] As the number of Israeli settlers in the West Bank grew, the military expressed great reluctance at having to enforce the law against Israeli citizens and delegated this authority to the Israel police. While such delegation does not relieve the IDF of its duty to enforce the law in the West Bank, when soldiers are called upon to intervene in settler attacks on Palestinians, they often claim that the police should be called.[451]

Despite official reports, and remarks in judgments of the Supreme Court, the failure to protect the Palestinians from settler violence continues. Credible NGO reports criticise this failure time and again.[452] There has been only one change, and not for the better. In the past, decision-makers confronted with the phenomenon of settler violence would be ill at ease. Since the establishment in December 2022 of the present government headed by Prime Minister Netanyahu, which includes the most extreme elements in Israeli society, settler violence has received support from politicians, including members of the Cabinet.[453]

---

450 Eilat Maoz, *Living Law: Police and Sovereignty in an Occupation Regime* (Van Leer Institute Press 2020) 65. Maoz reports a case in which the representative of settlers who were about to be evacuated by the military applied to a Supreme Court judge for an injunction to stop the evacuation on the grounds that the police should be dealing with the matter, not the military. The judge rejected the application.

451 According to a press report, in a Cabinet meeting that took place in January 2022 the Minister of Internal Security complained that while soldiers in the West Bank had the same powers as the police to detain Israelis involved in nationalist crimes, they were not using them. The Chief of Staff denied that the soldiers possessed such powers. Barak Ravid, 'Confrontation between Minister Bar-Lev and Kochavi over the authority of soldiers to act against settlers who attack Palestinians' *Walla* (31 January 2022) <https://news.walla.co.il/item/3486128> [in Hebrew] accessed 16 January 2025.

452 Yesh Din, 'Law Enforcement on Israeli Civilians in the West Bank (Settler Violence)' (December 2022) <https://s3.eu-west-1.amazonaws.com/files.yesh-din.org/law+data+dec+22/Law+data+22+ENG.pdf>; B'Tselem, 'Settler Violence = State Violence' (updating list) <https://www.btselem.org/settler_violence_updates_list> accessed 16 January 2025. Also see Maoz (n 450).

453 David Kretzmer and Limor Yehuda, 'Red Alert: Who Will Protect the Palestinians?' *Just Security* (27 March 2023) <https://www.justsecurity.org/85693/red-alert-who-will-protect-the-palestinians> accessed 19 January 2025. Also see report by TOI Staff, 'Ben Gvir praises settler who killed Palestinian in clash: "Should get medal of honor"' *The Times of Israel* (6 August 2023) <https://www.timesofisrael.com/ben-gvir-praises-settler-who-killed-palestinian-in-clash-should-get-medal-of-honor/> accessed 16 January 2025 (Minister of National Security praises settler arrested on charge of killing a Palestinian in a recent incident).

Since the Hamas attack of 7 October 2023 and the subsequent war in Gaza, incidents of settler violence have increased and the lax law enforcement against settlers continues.[454] As representatives of the extreme settlers now fulfil major posts in the government the chances of any change are negligible.

In his final judgment before retiring from the Supreme Court, Deputy President of the Court Salim Joubran stated:

> The Palestinian inhabitants of the Area are not like any other group of individuals who are subject to this or that administrative authority. We are speaking of protected persons under international law, who as such are entitled to special protection in a wide range of spheres, including the sphere of private property...Notwithstanding these provisions, the

454 For a devasting investigative report on the settler violence see Ronen Bergman and Mark Mazzetti, 'The Unpunished: How Extremists Took Over Israel' *The New York Times Magazine* (16 May 2024) <https://www.nytimes.com/2024/05/16/magazine/israel-west-bank-settler-violence-impunity.html?unlocked_article_code=1.GU4.Wdqq.W0ZOr-DzLvHz> accessed 16 January 2025. According to an NGO report, 2023 was the most violent year for West Bank settler attacks: *Times of Israel* 1 January 2024 <https://www.timesofisrael.com/2023-most-violent-year-for-west-bank-settler-attacks-watchdog-says/> accessed 28 January 2025. At the time of writing the violence settler continues without abatement: Hagar Shizaf, 'The attacks of settlers were preceded by calls in the social media, but once again the Palestinians were left without protection' *Haaretz* 21 January 2025 <https://www.haaretz.co.il/news/politics/2025-01-21/ty-article-smagazine/.premium/00000194-88c5-df25-a19e-cdcd05d00000> accessed 28 January 2025; Hagar Shizaf, 'During the Weekend Tens of Settlers attacked Palestinians and Soldiers in Two Places in the West Bank' *Haaretz* 16 Feb 2025 < https://www.haaretz.co.il/news/politics/2025-02-16/ty-article/00000195-0e1f-d00a-adfd-6edfc7370000 > accessed 15 April 2025 (In the second instance settlers set fire to houses and set dogs against local residents, but when soldiers arrived on the scene they did not arrest anyone); Nir Hasson, 'Witnesses: Settlers Attacked Residents in a Village in Msafa Yatta; More that 20 Palestinians were Arrested', *Haaretz* 28 March 2025 <https://www.haaretz.co.il/news/politics/2025-03-28/ty-article/.premium/00000195-dc43-da7e-adb7-fddb29c20000> accessed 15 April 2025. (Typically, in this case all the Palestinian men in the village were arrested while not one settler was arrested, although the authorities could easily have known from which settlement the settlers who attacked the Palestinians came). Also see Yesh Din, 'Data Sheet: Law Enforcement on Israeli Civilians in the West Bank [Settler Violence], 2005-2024' 16 Jan 2025 <https://www.yesh-din.org/en/data-sheet-law-enforcement-on-israeli-civilians-in-the-west-bank-settler-violence-2005-2024/> accessed 15 April 2025; B'Tselem, 'March 2025: Settler violence escalates with help from the Israeli military' 9 April 2025 < https://www.btselem.org/video/20250490_march_2025_settler_violence_escalates_with_help_from_the_israeli_military#full> accessed 15 April 2025.

> protected persons are inherently in an inferior position to that of the Israeli settlers in the Area, who are full citizens with equal rights in the State of Israel.[455]

This is a sad recognition of the reality in the West Bank following the massive introduction of Israeli settlers into the occupied territory. The consistent failure of the IDF to protect Palestinians in the West Bank from settler violence is a reflection of the Palestinians' "inherently inferior position." It is also a reflection of the "victory" of politics over law. The politics we are referring to are the politics of the most extreme messianic and nationalistic elements in Israeli society. From fringe elements they are now in power. International law, and indeed legal values and principles in general, are anathema to them.

455 *Ziada* case (n 298) para 116.

Chapter 8: Politics Rather Than Law

8.1 Developments since December 2022

Since the occupation began there has been a clear disparity between the regime of belligerent occupation, which according to the international community and the Supreme Court of Israel, is the legal regime that applies to Israel's actions in the West Bank, and the actual policies and practices of the government. At the same time the veneer of belligerent occupation was maintained. Legal powers were in the hands of the military commander in the West Bank, and the Civil Administration, the branch of the military government in charge of civilian (as opposed to military) matters, was headed by a senior military officer. Legal advice to the military commander and to the Civil Administration was provided by a department in the IDF MAG's office that dealt with the West Bank.[456]

The formal policy principles that the new government formed by PM Netanyahu in December 2022 adopted and presented to the Knesset, and the coalition agreement between Netanyahu's Likud party and the party of Minister of Finance Smotrich, reflect a decision to abandon even formal commitment to the norms of belligerent occupation. The said agreement commits the parties to a policy that strives for annexation of the West Bank, in flagrant violation of international law.

In order to appreciate the full implications of this move, one must consider an article published in 2017 in which Smotrich presented his plan for decisive action to "resolve" the conflict with the Palestinians. Smotrich claimed that his plan is not based solely on his religious belief in the divine

---

456 The task of this department is described as follows: "The Department of the Legal Advisor to the Region of Judea and Samaria (the West Bank, or the Area) is tasked with providing legal advice to the General Officer Commanding of the Central Command, and to the relevant entities operating under their authority, in order to assist in fulfilling their functions while preserving the security of the area, public order and the rule of law. The department advises the Central Command Headquarters and its divisions, as well as the Civil Administration of Judea and Samaria and the various District Coordination and Liaison Offices. The department also assists the Israel Police, the Israel Border Police, the Israeli Security Agency and the various governmental ministries concerning the law in Judea and Samaria." <https://www.idf.il/en/mini-sites/military-advocate-general-s-corps/department-of-the-legal-advisor-to-the-region-of-judea-and-samaria/> accessed 15 January 2025.

promise of the whole land of Israel exclusively to the Jewish people, and that non-believers can support the plan too. There is no doubt, however, that a "religious" world view of Jewish exclusivity and divine providence lies at the basis of the plan. This view is reflected in the terms of the coalition agreement between the Smotrich's Religious Zionist Party and the Likud that will be discussed below. That agreement states that the "belief" in the natural right of the Jewish people to the Land of Israel means that the sovereignty of the State of Israel should be extended to the Occupied Territories.

Smotrich's plan, which I have termed the "Subdual Plan"[457] is based on a number of assumptions and measures:

1. Until now the policy of successive Israeli governments has been to "manage" the conflict with the Palestinians until such time as an agreed political solution will be reached. As there is no chance of any such agreement that would answer the minimal demands even of the left in Israel and of Palestinians, the time has come for decisive action, to "resolve" the conflict.
2. The two-state solution was never a viable option and is certainly not an option now. There is no room for two national movements in the territory of the Land of Israel. Hence the only solution for those who support the continued existence of the Jewish state is to destroy any illusions that the Palestinians could at any stage realize national aspirations in this land. Palestinians who continue to live here will only be allowed to continue to do so if they waive their national aspirations and are prepared to live as individuals in the Jewish state.
3. Implementation of the plan involves a number of stages. The first is to increase Jewish settlement in the West Bank by hundreds of thousands. This will be carried out on what is termed "state land" (as we saw above, a misnomer for government property or public land).
4. The Palestinian residents of the occupied territories will have to choose between three possibilities:
   a. Emigration to surrounding Arab states or other countries with material help from the government of Israel;
   b. Waiving any national aspirations and expressing a willingness to live as individual subjects in the Jewish state, who will enjoy civil liberties

457 Bezalel Smotrich, 'The Subdual Plan: The Key to Peace is in the Hands of the Right' (2017) 6 *Hashiloah* 81 <https://hashiloach.org.il/wp-content/uploads/2019/12/hashiloach-6-all-web.pdf> [in Hebrew] accessed 16 January 2025. The plan is described in David Kretzmer (n 363).

but will not acquire citizenship and will not be entitled to vote in national elections;

c. Those who choose to oppose continued Israeli rule will be crushed with force. The army will go to war and defeat them. "Given a decisive and unambiguous political directive [the IDF] will without doubt know how to defeat the terrorists in a short time; to kill those who need to be killed, to collect all weapons to the last bullet and to restore security to the citizens of Israel."[458]

It is not my intention in the present context to assess the political feasibility, nor the legal and moral legitimacy, of the "Subdual Plan". What I wish to show now is the connection between this plan and clauses in the guiding principles of the present government and in the coalition agreement between the Likud and the Religious Zionist party.

Under a clause in the coalition agreement, Smotrich was appointed not only as Minister of Finance, but also as a second minister in the Ministry of Defence. In this capacity, he, rather than the military, has control over all civilian matters in the West Bank, including the issue of settlements and unauthorized outposts and land use (at least in Area C).[459] In May 2024 a formal legal order was promulgated appointing a civilian official in Smotrich's department as "assistant head of the Civil Administration" who will have all the powers of the Civil Administration.[460]

Under the coalition agreement all unauthorised outposts are to be regularized. It was reported in July 2024 that the Minister of Finance Smotrich gave instructions to government ministries to provide services and infrastructure in outposts that had not been regularized.[461]

---

458 ibid 97.

459 For the argument that this move is incompatible with the international law of belligerent occupation, under which control of the occupied territory is in the hands of the military see Michal Saliternik and Ronit Levine-Schnur, 'This Decision by Israel is as Dramatic as Attempts at Constitutional Change' *Ha'aretz* (22 June 2023) <https://www.haaretz.com/israel-news/2023-06-22/ty-article-opinion/.premium/this-decision-by-israel-is-as-dramatic-as-attempts-at-constitutional-change/00000188-e282-df52-a79d-fea3d6150000> accessed 16 January 2025.

460 *Order Concerning Establishment of the Civil Administration (Amendment no. 33) (Order no. 2195)*, 2024.

461 Hagar Shizaf and Jonathan Lis, 'Smotrich directed government ministries to provide services and infrastructure to outposts that have not yet been regularized' *Ha'aretz* (20 April 2024) <https://www.haaretz.co.il/news/politics/2024-04-20/ty-article/0000018e-fcfb-d64a-a9ae-fcfba44c0000> accessed 16 January 2025.

The government's guiding principles attached to all the coalition agreements signed between the Likud and the other parties in the governing coalition, state that the "Jewish people have the sole and indisputable right over all parts of the Land of Israel" and that the government will promote and develop settlement in all areas, including Judea and Samaria.[462] The coalition agreement with the "Religious Zionist" party states that the prime minister will further creation and promotion of a policy under which Israeli sovereignty will be applied to Judea and Samaria "while choosing the time and considering all the national and international interests of the State of Israel." The guiding principles and coalition agreements also include commitments to do the following:

a. regularize all "young settlements", and all neighbourhoods in existing settlements that were built without government and planning approval. To the extent that this is not possible under the existing law, legislation will be adopted to allow it;
b. ensure the existence and continued development of the Jewish settlement in the city of Hebron;
c. amend the Cabinet decision that requires Cabinet approval for all new settlements;
d. regulate and define the status and function of the Settlement Division of the World Zionist Organization (the main body behind Jewish settlement in the West Bank), and to provide this body with a budget of 750 million shekels;
e. adopt a five-year plan for settlement in Judea and Samaria;
f. cancel the disengagement from a number of settlements in the northern part of the West Bank, that was part of the Disengagement from Gaza, implemented by the Sharon government in 2005.

All these commitments and declarations, when combined with the power given to Bezalel Smotrich over the purse-strings and over all civilian matters in the West Bank, mean that all pretences of adherence to international law have been cast aside. Many parts of the above policy and coalition agreements have already been implemented. A law was enacted revoking

462 All the coalition agreements to which the government's guiding principles are attached are available on the Knesset's homepage: <https://main.knesset.gov.il/mk/government/pages/governments.aspx?govId=37> [in Hebrew] accessed 16 January 2025.

the "Disengagement" that was applied in an area in the northern part of the West Bank,[463] and Israeli settlements have been established in the area.[464]

Political interests have prevailed. It remains to be seen to what extent the Supreme Court will be prepared to go along with this change in policy. How will it relate to arguments that actions of the authorities in the West Bank are incompatible with the regime of belligerent occupation? Recent judgments of the Court are not encouraging.[465]

8.2 Politics Prevail

Let me now summarize the developments that have led to the ultimate victory of domestic politics over law.

The international law of belligerent occupation was the legal regime that was instituted in the newly occupied territories when the occupation began in June 1967. The framework for this regime had been prepared by the MAG's office as a contingency plan before war broke out, and the framework was set in place as soon as the IDF gained control over territories that had not been part of Israel's territory before the war. This regime rests on a military government headed by a senior military officer who ostensibly concentrates all governmental powers in his hands. In the first few months of the occupation military lawyers and the legal adviser of the Ministry of Foreign Affairs were committed to this regime and provided legal advice that was consistent with it. They warned against actions of the military that were not compatible with the regime, and the Prime Minister even requested a legal opinion on whether settlements in the West Bank for Israeli civilians was lawful.

The initial commitment of lawyers to this regime was not shared by many politicians, public figures and senior civil servants. Some objected

---

463 *Law Implementing the Disengagement Plan (Amendment no. 7)*, 2023.

464 The settlements were established after the minister of defence, relying on the new law, lifted restrictions on establishing settlements in the area: ToI Staff, 'Gallant lifts order barring access to evacuated settlements in northern West Bank' *The Times of Israel* (22 May 2024) <https://www.timesofisrael.com/gallant-lifts-order-barring-access-to-evacuated-settlements-in-northern-west-bank/> accessed 16 January 2025.

465 See *Abu Aram case* (n 98) and the criticism of this judgment by Ben-Naftali and Diamond (n 98); HCJ 58245/04 *Hebron Municipality* v *State of Israel* (25 Nov 2024) (Court relies on assurance of the authorities that they will remove a road that had been illegally built by settlers on land of the Hebron Municipality and does not issue an order for them to do so).

to the very notion of "occupation", which has a pejorative connation.[466] Others were wary of the constraints that the regime of belligerent occupation imposes on the occupying power. Still others held nationalistic or even messianic views relating to the connection between the Jewish people and their ancient homeland.

A few days after the occupation began persons and groups in the political arena and in civil society began promoting the view that the newly occupied territories that were part of the historical Land of Israel had been liberated, not occupied.[467] Within a short time a movement arose that promoted the idea that Israeli territory should now consist of the whole of the Greater Land of Israel, meaning that Israel should maintain permanent control over the West Bank and Gaza.[468] It was only a matter of time before lawyers who subscribed to these views began promoting legal arguments to support them.

The first step in laying the legal foundations for the argument that the West Bank was not occupied territory, and that Israel had a legitimate claim to sovereignty over the area, was laid by a professor of international law. He argued that since Jordan was not a legitimate sovereign in the West Bank the part of the law of occupation whose purpose is to protect the missing sovereign of the territory does not apply. Even though he stated expressly that the humanitarian norms that apply in occupied territory apply in the West Bank, his argument was cited by the Attorney General as grounds for denying *de* jure application of the Forth Geneva Convention in the area. This position has since remained the official position of the Government of Israel.

When the first petitions were submitted to the Supreme Court challenging actions of the military commander in the West Bank on grounds of international law, government lawyers were faced with a dilemma. Since they accepted that in its role as the High Court of Justice the Supreme Court has jurisdiction to entertain these petitions, they had to contend with the substantive legal arguments raised by the petitioners. On the one hand,

---

466 Paul Bremer, the Administrator of the Coalition Provisional Authority in Iraq is reported to have said that occupation is "an ugly word"; cited in Peter MR Stirk (n 2) 3.

467 The first public statements that "we liberated, we did not occupy" were published in the press in June 1967. Some of these statements are printed in Avi Katzman (ed), *Controversies: 60 Momentous Debated in the Hebrew Press from 1918 to 2008* (Am Oved 2008) 242-245.

468 The Movement for the Greater Israel published its call for Israel to extend its sovereignty over the West Bank and Gaza on 22 September 1967: Katzman, ibid 244.

they did not want to depart from the view that the Geneva Convention, and possibly the whole corpus of the law of belligerent occupation, do not apply to Israel's actions in the West Bank. On the other hand, since Israel had not purported to apply its laws in the West Bank (with the exception of East Jerusalem), they had no other legal framework to explain the military commander's status in the area. Furthermore, in defending the military's actions they were reluctant to hide behind formalistic arguments, lest their approach be interpreted as admission that these actions were incompatible with international law. They therefore adopted what I have termed the "pragmatic approach", which involved asking the Court to consider the petitioners' arguments on the merits without ruling that the law of belligerent occupation applies *de jure*.

Most judges on the Court were prepared initially to go along with this pragmatic approach. However, the approach had its limits. Firstly, the approach was tenable only when the military authorities accepted limitations on their powers under the prevailing local law; it was not tenable when the authorities themselves relied on the law of belligerent occupation for their very power to violate rights of the local population, such as their right to property. Secondly, as the Court revealed in the *Ha'etzni* case,[469] the Court had to provide a legal basis for the powers of the military commander. Absent any other legal framework it turned to the customary international law of belligerent occupation, as reflected in the Hague Regulations. Finally, as time passed and the Court based numerous judgments on the law of belligerent occupation, it could not make an about turn and rule that this law did not in fact apply in the West Bank. Hence it was not long before the Court ruled categorically that the legal regime in the West Bank is the regime of belligerent occupation. The only caveat was that the Court itself would only enforce norms of that regime that are part of customary international law. When arguing before the Court, government lawyers have accepted this approach and have consistently based their defence of government actions on customary international law, as reflected in the Hague Regulations Respecting the Laws and Customs of War on Land, 1907.

The Supreme Court's jurisdiction as the High Court of Justice plays a central role in Israel's political and legal system. This has both positive and negative effects. On the positive side, review by the High Court of Justice is the main, and often the only, constraint on abuse of governmental power

469 *Ha'etzni* case (n 251).

in a parliamentary system in which the executive branch of government usually has *de facto* control over the majority in the Knesset. Despite the criticism that Yaël Ronen and I, and many other scholars, have voiced over the Court's record in cases relating to the Occupied Territories, there can be little doubt that if the Court had not reviewed cases from these territories, there would have been far more arbitrariness in the actions of the authorities there. The negative side of the Court's role is that there is a widely held view that if the Court dismisses a petition, whether on the merits or on other grounds, the action challenged in the petition is not only legal, but also justified morally. This view has been internalized by government lawyers so that the only real question that bothers them in assessing the legality of a government policy or practice is whether it will stand up to judicial review by the Supreme Court. A clear manifestation of this view was the discussion in the Cabinet after the Court's judgment in the *Elon Moreh* case. In that case the Court refused to consider the argument that establishing settlements for civilians of the occupying power is incompatible with Article 49 (6) of the Geneva Convention, since it held that this provision does not reflect customary law. Justice Witkon saw fit to state that his refusal to consider the argument should not be interpreted as agreement with the one or other of the parties. Yet in the Cabinet discussion the only point of the judgment mentioned by the Attorney General was the use of private land that ostensibly had been seized for military needs to build a civilian settlement. The Attorney General even went further and said that if the government wished to establish settlements it should do so on government land. He made no mention of the fact that Justice Witkon had stated expressly that the Geneva Convention applies in the West Bank and that the Court had left open the question of whether establishing settlements was compatible with the Convention.

In light of the view that legality is taken to mean that the action will not be overruled by the Supreme Court, we must consider three principles that have guided the Court: it will not enforce treaty law; not all the provisions of the Fourth Geneva Convention reflect customary international law; and the legality of settlements under international law is not justiciable. The first two principles have meant that the authorities can largely ignore the Geneva Convention when assessing the legality of governmental action. The third ruling has meant that since Theodor Meron wrote his opinion on the issue in September 1967, the settlement policy of the government in the Occupied Territories has not met with objections of government lawyers. This has helped the government to ignore the intense criticism of this policy that has been voiced by the UN Security Council and many states that are not generally unfriendly towards Israel.

In examining the role of lawyers in facilitating the abandonment of the admittedly partial commitment to the international law of belligerent occupation I am fully aware that we have little knowledge of cases in which government lawyers managed to halt or mitigate planned actions of the authorities. We do know of cases in which lawyers in the Attorney General's office refused to defend specific measures of the government in court.[470] We also know of opinions of the Attorney General that overruled decisions of governmental authorities[471] or prevented government actions.[472] There might well have been many more cases, of which we have no knowledge, in which lawyers in the IDF or the government ministries, forced the authorities to halt or revoke measures or actions. Without denying that government lawyers may have had a restraining influence over actions of the authorities in the West Bank, I shall now relate to cases in which lawyers were instrumental in providing the government with the legal basis to pursue policies the legality of which under international law is highly questionable.

It is clear that the establishment of Israeli settlements in the West Bank is the most problematic policy of Israel. The international community and most experts in international law agree that establishment of such settlements violates international law. The settlements paved the way for the *de facto* annexation of Area C in the West Bank, in contravention of the prohibition on acquisition of territory by force, for denial of the right of the Palestinians to self-determination, and for violation of many other rights of the local population. Establishment of the settlements has also led to the existence of two separate ethnic groups in the West Bank, who are subject to different legal regimes, thus leading to the opinion of the ICJ that

---

470 See the note by Dorit Beinisch (n 278).

471 In 1989 the planning bodies in Israel decided on a new cemetery for Israeli residents that would be located in the West Bank. When the Peace Now movement petitioned the Supreme Court challenging the legality of the decision the Attorney General's office informed the Court that having examined the issue it was of the opinion that "it is forbidden to establish a cemetery for the residents of Jerusalem in Judea and Samaria": <https://peacenow.org.il/modiin-illit-cemetery> [in Hebrew] accessed 16 January 2025. As a result the plan was abandoned and the existing cemetery in Jerusalem was expanded.

472 See the opinion of the Attorney General of 12 May 1980 (n 299), in which he held that private land may not be expropriated for building new settlements.

Israel is liable for breaching the prohibition of racial discrimination, if not of apartheid. What was the contribution of lawyers to this policy?

Lawyers have given backing to the settlement policy of the governments that have held power since 1967 in a number of ways. As we saw above, Yehuda Blum's argument about Jordan's lack of sovereignty in the West Bank when it was occupied by Israel was cited as the basis for claiming that GCIV does not apply to the occupation of that area. It would seem that one of the reasons that this argument was raised was to avoid the claim that by establishing settlements Israel was violating Article 49(6) of the Convention. Strength for the connection between the argument on non-application of the Convention and the issue of settlements may be found in the fact that the provision in the military order obliging military courts in the West Bank to respect the Convention was revoked soon after the legal adviser of the Ministry of Foreign Affairs had submitted his opinion that establishment of settlements would be seen as a violation of Article 49(6).

The non-application of the whole Geneva Convention was not the only argument raised to refute the claim that Israel was violating its international obligation set out in Article 49(6) of the Convention. Another argument, still raised in government quarters, is that the word "transfer" in Article 49(6)[473] includes an element of coercion, and since all settlers settle in the West Bank of their own free will, the Article does not apply to Israeli settlements.[474] This argument is unconvincing. Firstly, paragraph 1 in Article 49 refers to "forcible transfers". It should be clear then that if in another paragraph in the same article there is a reference merely to "transfer" the conclusion is that in that paragraph the transfer does not have to be forcible. Secondly, and possibly more importantly, the object of the Geneva Convention is to protect inhabitants of the occupied territory ("protected persons") and not citizens of the occupying power.[475] From the point of view of the local inhabitants it makes little difference whether civilians of

473 "The occupying power shall not deport or transfer parts of its own civilian population into the territory it occupies."

474 This view is presented in an item entitled 'Israeli settlements and international law' on the website of the Israel Ministry of Foreign Affairs: <https://www.gov.il/en/pages/israeli-settlement-and-international-law> accessed 16 January 2025. It was also raised by Eugene Rostow, 'Correspondence' (n 154) 719.

475 *Commentary on Geneva Convention (IV) Relative to the Protection of Civilians in Times of War* (JS Pictet ed, 1958) 46, para 1. In relating to the definition of "protected persons" which excludes nationals of the occupying power, the Commentary states: "The Convention thus remains remains faithful to a recognized principle of international law: it does not interfere in a State's relations with its own nationals."

the occupying power settle in their territory willingly or against their will. This should have been apparent to the lawyers who raised the argument that Article 49(6) requires an element of coercion.

Lawyers provided legitimacy for the settlement project in other ways too. As we saw above, after the *Elon Moreh* judgment, the Attorney General told the government that if it wished to continue with the settlement policy it could do so on government property. No mention was made of the fact that establishing settlements on such land would involve violation of international law, and was also incompatible with the "insuperable legal obstacle" presented by Justice Landau in the *Elon Moreh* judgment.[476] Lawyers never warned the government that using public land for the benefit of nationals of the occupying power is incompatible with customary international law, as reflected in Article 55 of the Hague Regulations. Subsequently lawyers played a major role in widening the definition of "government property" and in locating uncultivated land that could be used for settlements.[477] Despite the legal opinion of the MAG's office of July 1967 regarding the legal problems involved in establishing "fire zones" in occupied territory, lawyers lent their hand to seizure of vast tracts of land in the West Bank for such zones. They also defended such seizure in court, even when evidence was produced that the motivation for seizure of land for a fire zone was simply to seize the land.[478]

The role lawyers played in paving the way for the government to depart from the international law of belligerent occupation and to implement policies that are incompatible with that law raises searching questions regarding the role of government lawyers and legal advisers. Are they first and foremost "gatekeepers" whose primary task is to ensure that governmental

---

476 n 165.

477 The leading figure in the location of uncultivated land to be used for settlements was the Deputy Attorney General in the Ministry of Justice. In a lecture to the Tel Aviv branch of the Israel Bar Association she described the procedure involved: Plia Abeck, *Lands in Judea and Samaria* (Israel Bar Association 1985).

478 *Abu Aram* case (n 98). In a meeting with IDF representatives Ariel Sharon, at the time the minister in charge of settlement, stated that there was an interest in the military declaring firing zones, so that Palestinians could not take control over the land. Minutes of the Joint Settlement Committee of the Government and the World Zionist Organization (12 July 1981) <https://www.akevot.org.il/wp-content/uploads/2020/08/1981-07-12-%D7%95%D7%A2%D7%93%D7%AA-%D7%A9%D7%A8%D7%99%D7%9D-%D7%9C%D7%94%D7%AA%D7%99%D7%A9%D7%91%D7%95%D7%AA-%D7%A4%D7%A8%D7%95%D7%98%D7%95%D7%A7%D7%95%D7%9C-%D7%9E%D7%9C%D7%90-%D7%9E%D7%9B%D7%95%D7%9F-%D7%A2%D7%A7%D7%91%D7%95%D7%AA.pdf> [in Hebrew] accessed 16 January 2025.

authorities comply with the law, which in the case of occupied territory is clearly the international law of belligerent occupation? Or are they more like lawyers who advise private clients by trying for find the best possible legal arguments to support their interests? And even if they see themselves as "gatekeepers", what compromises should they make, when they realise that if they take a "hard line" their advice may be ignored, especially if accepting their opinion means that the government will have to abandon a major policy? Was this behind the Attorney General's advice after the *Elon Moreh* case? Given the ideological and political commitment of Menachem Begin and his government to settlement in the West Bank, did he waive mention of the limits of international law on such settlement because he knew it would simply be ignored?[479] The reader will recall that the Eshkol Labour government, which did not have the same strong ideological commitment to settlement as the Begin Likud government, had ignored Meron's legal opinion that establishing settlements would be regarded as a violation of GCIV.

The role of the Supreme Court in explicitly or implicitly granting legitimacy to various policies and practices of the authorities was discussed above. It is, of course, not possible to say what the position in the West Bank would have been today if the Court had declined to exercise jurisdiction over acts of the military in the Occupied Territories, or if had adopted a more rigorous approach in interpreting and applying the norms of international law. Meir Shamgar, Chief Justice from 1983-1995, wrote many of the judgements relating to the Occupied Territories. In his auto-

---

479 In two meetings of the Cabinet that dealt with the implications of the *Elon Moreh* case (n 151) many of the ministers who spoke stressed the deep commitment of the government to establishment of settlements in the West Bank. Minutes of Cabinet meeting no. 7/5740 (28 October 1979) (on file with author); Minutes of Cabinet meeting no. 8/5740 (n 374). In the latter meeting one of the ministers suggested establishing a team of lawyers who supported the settlement policy in order to advise the government how to proceed in implementing the policy. The Attorney General reacted strongly to this proposal. He stressed that legal advice to the government would be provided by his office, that nobody knew what his political opinion was, and that legal advisers would not be chosen according to their supposed political opinions. In the same meeting one of the ministers was highly critical of the way the Attorney General's office had defended the government in the *Elon Moreh* case. When challenged by the Attorney General to provide details of his criticism he refrained from doing so. Another minister had been one of the founders of the *Gush Emunim* movement that was behind the Elon Moreh settlement. It is not inconceivable that in this environment had the Attorney General told the Cabinet that settlements were incompatible with international law the Cabinet would have asked him to resign.

biography, published ten years after he retired from the Court, Shamgar was quite candid that he did not regard his judicial role in this context as challenging government policies, but in granting a remedy to an individual whose rights had been violated. The implication was that justice had to be provided within the context of government policies, even if their legality was dubious.

Judicial review by the Supreme Court of Israel over the acts of the military in occupied territory was regarded as an important development that was unique in the annals of belligerent occupation.[480] But the record of the Supreme Court in exercising this review raises searching questions about the limitations of such review. Can a national court of an occupying power be expected to divorce itself from the political context in which it operates? Can it take a stand on matters of foreign and security policy that differs from that of the executive branch of government, especially when that policy is subject to intense international criticism? Like national courts in other democratic countries, judges in Israel are independent; but they are not, and cannot be, neutral in issues relating to a long-term and bitter conflict between their own country and another people.[481] These factors expose the inherent shortcomings of judicial review by the courts of the occupying power. It is clear to me that despite these shortcomings making the military authorities accountable to an external judicial body is of crucial importance. Nevertheless, the Israeli experience reveals that such review is neither a panacea nor a mechanism that ensures the rule of law in occupied territory.

480 Eli Nathan, 'The Power of Supervision of the High Court of Justice over Military Government' in Meir Shamgar (n 96) 109. Before the Supreme Court of Israel held that it had jurisdiction to review the actions of the military in occupied territory there was a least one case in which a national court held that it did not have such jurisdiction: *In re Société Bonduelle et Cie* (1951) 18 *International Law Reports* 573.

481 On the neutrality, as opposed to independence, of judges in democratic societies see J.A.G Griffith, *The Politics of the Judiciary* (4th edn, HarperCollins 1991) 269.

Chapter 9: Concluding Observations

While military lawyers originally assumed that any territory taken in war by Israel would be territory to which the international law of belligerent occupation applies, soon after Israel gained control over the West Bank it became apparent that this assumption was incompatible with the political designs of the Israeli government. The attachment to the law of belligerent occupation was not abandoned, but was restricted to discourse in legal fora, and even there it was applied in a selective manner. Lawyers were instrumental in manipulating the law in order to cater to the government's political interests. What was created amounts in effect to a distinction between the territory and its people. The territory itself is not regarded as occupied, but the Palestinian inhabitants of the territory are subject to a regime of belligerent occupation. In the Introduction I mentioned the remark of Prime Minister Levy Eshkol when describing the results of the 1967 Six Day War. Israel had received a wonderful dowry, but it was not interested in the bride. The distinction between the land and the people rests on this perception.

Not only is there a distinction between territory and people. There is also a distinction between the Palestinian inhabitants and the Israeli settlers. The latter are formally subject to the authority of the military commander of the area, but they live and operate under a legal regime that is entirely different from the regime of belligerent occupation that applies to the Palestinian inhabitants.[482] Part of the legal distinction between the status and rights of the two populations living in the West Bank is a function of military orders and Knesset legislation; other parts are a direct consequence of judgments of the Supreme Court.

Given the above developments, it is not surprising that notwithstanding the internationally recognized status of the West Bank as occupied territory, in the last few years there has been a growing literature on the actual nature of the regime there. One issue is whether, despite the fact that Israel has not formally annexed the territory, the territory has been annexed *de facto*, in contravention of the prohibition in international law of acquiring

482 See Association of Civil Rights in Israel, 'One Rule: Two Legal Systems' (n 431).

territory through use of force.[483] In its Advisory Opinion of July 2024, the International Court of Justice opined that "policies, practices or other measures that are such as to bring the occupied territory under the occupying Power's permanent control constitute acts of annexation."[484] It proceeded to hold that Israel's policies and practices amount to annexation of large parts of the West Bank.[485]

The most recent move by the present government has been promulgation of a military order transferring the powers on civilian matters in the West Bank from the Civil Administration, a branch of the military government headed by a senior military officer, to an official in the ministry of defence. This official is under the authority of the minister of finance, one of the most extreme members of the present government who represents the settlers and believes in formal annexation of the territory. This move supports the view of the ICJ on annexation.

One has to question the responsibility of lawyers, especially those advising the government and defending its actions in court. There were lawyers in the public service who refused to compromise their principles and even refused on occasion to defend government decisions in court. But there were many others who advanced spurious legal arguments in order to lend support to government policies and decisions. At the present juncture, when Israel and Israel's leaders are being called to account before various international judicial fora, one has to ask whether Israel is paying the price for this.

The existence of a large number of Israeli settlers in the West Bank makes it virtually impossible to reach an agreement on a two-state solution, or to implement such a solution were it to be reached. In fact the vision of such a solution, still favoured by the international community, has become an illusion. It does not seem to me that the present situation, in which Palestinians in the West Bank do not have political rights in the state that rules them, can continue indefinitely. If the two-state solution is no longer tenable, another solution will have to be found that will allow all persons in Israel and the West Bank to enjoy equal civil and political rights.

Can one learn anything from the West Bank case as regards the international law of belligerent occupation? This law was developed in the

483 Ronit Levin-Schnur, Tamar Megiddo, and Yael Berda, *A Theory of Annexation* (23 January 2023) available at <https://papers.ssrn.com/sol3/papers.cfm?abstract_id=4330338> accessed 16 January 2025.

484 Advisory Opinion, *Occupied Palestinian Territory* (n 9) para 172.

485 Ibid. para 173.

19th Century and its fundamentals are still those enshrined in the Hague Regulations of 1907. We are living today in a totally different world than the world of 120 years ago. As mentioned in the Introduction, few if any occupying powers in the last fifty years have been prepared to recognize that this law applies in the territory they occupied. Israel's occupation in the West Bank is one highly ambiguous exception. But as we have seen, in this exceptional case the acceptance of the law of occupation was half-hearted, and the occupying state's actions and policies have been incompatible with that law.

Law, especially international law, cannot be divorced from politics.[486] Does the West Bank case show that there cannot be a belligerent occupation (especially one that continues for more than a very short period of time) that is run by the military in a manner removed from the political interests of its own government? If the answer is positive, it is far from clear what can be done about it.

The law of belligerent occupation clearly rests on the assumption that the occupation will be short-lived. But it makes little provision for a case in which it becomes prolonged.[487] Clearly an occupying power cannot free itself from its legal obligations by drawing out the occupation. It should be recognised, however, that a situation in which people remain subject to a regime of belligerent occupation for an extended period during which they do not enjoy political rights in the society in which they live is incompatible with modern conceptions of universal human rights, that should apply to all human beings, whatever the legal status of the territory in which they reside.[488] At the same time it has been argued that attempts to solve this problem by applying universal human rights standards in occupied territory in which citizens of the occupying power live alongside the local

---

486 Martti Koskenniemi 'The Politics of International Law' (1990) 1 *European Journal of International Law* 4.

487 Art 6 of GCIV stipulates that in occupied territory the Convention will cease one year after the general close of military operations, though to the extent that the occupying power exercises the functions of government in such territory it will remain bound by certain provisions of the Convention. This one-year restriction was abolished by Art 3 of the 1977 Additional Protocol I to the Geneva Conventions of 1949, although it still applies to states that are not parties to the Additional Protocol. This has led to serious difficulties in interpretation and application of Art 6. See Ben-Naftali, Sfard and Viterbo (n 1).

488 In its *Wall Advisory Opinion* (n 82) the ICJ held that alongside its obligations under the law of belligerent occupation Israel is bound in its actions in the West Bank by its obligations under human rights treaties to which it is a party.

population may undermine the special protection that the law of belligerent occupation extends to the inhabitants of such territory.[489] Maybe the only possible conclusion is to recognise the limits of law, and to meet the victory of domestic politics over law with a victory of international politics over domestic politics.

In its Advisory Opinion of July 2024 the ICJ opined that Israel's continued presence in the West Bank is unlawful and that it is under an obligation to bring that presence to an end as rapidly as possible.[490] The Government of Israel simply rejected the Advisory Opinion, relying on the opinion of an Israeli professor of law who contests the status of the West Bank as occupied territory on the basis of the "Mandate argument".[491] Whatever one may think of the Advisory Opinion's legal analysis and conclusions, it would seem that the Opinion is a fine example of law flying in the face of political reality. As domestic politics have prevailed over law, what is needed now, more urgently than ever, is international pressure for a political arrangement between Israel and the Palestinians that will end the occupation and the conflict. While I have expressed my doubts here and elsewhere whether a two-state solution is still viable,[492] in the absence of a realistic alternative I can do no better than end this study by quoting the following statement of Judges Tomka, Abraham and Aurescu in their joint separate opinion in the Advisory Opinion case:

> For many decades, the Israeli and the Palestinian peoples have been in conflict - a conflict with many complex legal, political and historical aspects - related to the territory of Palestine, entrusted by mandate of the League of Nations to the United Kingdom in 1922. The rights of one cannot be exercised to the detriment of the rights of the other. The "two-State solution", required by successive Security Council resolutions... is the only one that can respond to the legitimate need for security of both Israel and Palestine. This solution can only arise from a comprehensive understanding reached through negotiations, which must take into account all rights and interests involved: the right of the Palestinian people to self-determination is not incompatible with that of Israel to

---

489 Gross (n 298).

490 Advisory Opinion, *Occupied Palestinian Territory* (n 9).

491 See note 160 above.

492 See Micheline Ishay and David Kretzmer, 'Reclaiming Human Rights: An Alternative Approach to the Israel-Palestine Conflict' in John Ehrenberg and Yoav Peled (eds) *Israel and Palestine: Alternative Perspectives on Statehood* (Rowman and Littlefield 2016) 77.

exist in security, while Palestine's right to security must also be taken into account. The right to self-determination and the right to security must be implemented simultaneously in order to achieve the coexistence of the two States, which will also mark the end of Israel's presence as an occupying Power in the Palestinian territory.[493]

493 Advisory Opinion, *Occupied Palestinian Territory* (n 9), joint separate opinion of Judges Tomka, Abraham and Aurescu, para.10.